The Last Voyage
Perform'd by de la Sale

A
JOURNAL
Of the LAST
VOYAGE
Perform'd by
Monſr. de la Sale,
TO THE
GULPH OF MEXICO,
To find out the
Mouth of the *Miſſiſipi* River;

CONTAINING,

An Account of the Settlements he endeavour'd to make on the Coaſt of the aforeſaid *Bay*, his unfortunate Death, and the Travels of his Companions for the Space of Eight Hundred Leagues acroſs that Inland Country of *America*, now call'd *Louiſiana*, (and given by the King of *France* to M. *Crozat*,)till they came into *Canada*.

Written in French *by Monſieur* JOUTEL,
A Commander in that Expedition;
And Tranſlated from the Edition juſt publiſh'd at Paris.

With an exaɛt Map of that vaſt Country, and a Copy of the *Letters Patents* granted by the K. of *France* to M. *Crozat*.

LONDON, Printed for *A. Bell* at the *Croſs-Keys* and *Bible* in *Cornbill*, *B. Lintott* at the *Croſs Keys* in *Fleet-ſtreet*, and *J. Baker* in *Pater-Noſter-Row*, 1714.

Great Americana

The Last Voyage
Perform'd by de la Sale

Henri Joutel

The Last Voyage
Perform'd by de la Sale

by Henri Joutel

READEX MICROPRINT

Foreword

A Journal of the Last Voyage Perform'd by Monsr. de la Sale, To The Gulph of Mexico, To find out the Mouth of the Mississippi River, by Henri Joutel, was first published in French in 1713, then translated into English and printed in 1714. Joutel described how La Salle, with Louis XIV's blessing, attempted to plant a colony at the mouth of the Mississippi and to extend French dominion over Louisiana.

Four ships carrying Joutel and the other members of La Salle's party sailed from La Rochelle in July, 1684. Trouble arose from the start with frequent clashes between La Salle and the naval commander, Monsieur de Beaujeu. When the expedition neared its goal, La Salle committed "an irretrieveable Error," in Joutel's words, by sailing past the Mississippi in the mistaken notion that it lay farther to the west. La Salle landed his settlers on the coast of what is now Texas.

The capture of one ship by the Spaniards, the return of another to France, and the shipwreck of two more, deprived La Salle of support by sea. The hardships suffered by the men, women, and children of the expedition were innumerable. Some wandered off, never to be heard from again; others fell to Indian attack, were eaten by alligators, or were lost in a variety of accidents; others succumbed to disease. The painfully slow progress of building Fort

St. Louis in the Matagorda Bay area of Texas discouraged the survivors, particularly with La Salle's repeated failures to locate "his fatal Mississippi River," as Joutel called it. Finally, La Salle determined to return to France by way of Canada to bring help. Leaving most of the settlers at Fort St. Louis, where they were later overrun by the Indians, he set out with a small band in January, 1687. However the "implacable Hatred" which his haughty manner had aroused among some of his followers resulted in his murder in March, 1687. Joutel, no party to the crime, lamented his commander's death "at a Time when he might entertain the greatest Hopes as the Reward of his Labours." Joutel and several companions eventually separated from the assassins and resumed their journey. Joutel has much to say about the countryside they passed through and about the Indians they encountered. He reached Quebec in August, 1688, and France, two months later. Accounts by Joutel and by others regarding La Salle's exploits alerted France and all Europe to the value of Louisiana. La Salle's failure made possible later French success in that area.

Joutel's *Journal*, as printed here, is an abridgment of the original by the Sieur de Mitchel. Mitchel's preface, together with other explanatory remarks, a map, and a copy of Louis XIV's instructions of 1712 for the government of Louisiana, are included in this edition. Marion A. Habig, "The Franciscan Père Marquette," *Franciscan Studies* (June, 1934), No. 13, pp. 270-271 provides additional information about the *Journal*.

THE

French BOOKSELLER

TO THE

READER.

THE *Manuſcript of this Journal hapning to fall into my Hands, and having ſhewn it to ſome Perſons well vers'd in theſe Affairs, they were of Opinion it deſerv'd to be printed; eſpecially at this Time, when Travels are ſo much in Requeſt, and in Regard this is now ſeaſonable, on Account of the Deſcription it gives of the famous River* Miſſiſipi *and of the Country of* Louiſiana, *where it is intended to make great Settlements. Beſides, this Relation is uncommon, curious and ingaging, both in Regard to the Honour and Advan-*

tage

tage of the Nation, for as much as it contains the Attempts and the bold and glorious Undertakings of our French *Adventurers, who not satisfied, like others, with discovering the Borders and Coasts of unknown Countries, proceed to penetrate into the Inland, through a thousand Dangers and Hazards of their Lives. Is it not very commendable in them, to make us fully acquainted with that great remaining Part of the World, which for so many Ages continued unknown to our Forefathers, till about two hundred Years ago* Christopher Columbus *discover'd it, and* Americus Vespusius *going over soon after, gave it his Name, causing it to be call'd* America? *One of those whom I desired to peruse this Manuscript, has a little polish'd it, pursuant to the Orders I receiv'd; and he having been a considerable Traveller, was a proper Person to judge of and put it into a Dress fit to appear in publick. The Letter he writ to me, being not only instructive, in Relation to the Journal, but of Use as a curious Supplement to it, I thought the inserting of it would be acceptable. It is as follows.*

SIR,

S I R,

I Return you your. Manuscript ; the Reading of it has reviv'd the Satisfaction I once took in my Travels ; it has oblig'd me to read over again those of several Persons, who have writ of *Canada*, and carry'd me in Imagination through those vast, barbarous and unknown Countries, with much more Ease and less Danger than was done by the Hero of this Relation. He certainly deserves that honourable Title, and having read his Adventures, I could not forbear saying with the Poet

> *Illi robur & æs triplex*
> *Circa Pectus erat.*

For what an extraordinary Strength, what a Vigour of Body and Mind was requisite for him to project, to undertake and to go thro' with so unusual, so bold and so difficult an Enterprize. A Discovery of above eight hundred Leagues of barbarous and unknown Countries, without any beaten Roads, without Towns, and without any of those Conveniencies, which render Travelling more easy in all

other

other Parts. All the Land-Carriage is re-
duc'd to walking afoot ; being often without any other Shoes but a Piece of a Bullock's Hide wrapp'd about the Feet ; carrying a Firelock, a Snapſack, Tools and
ſome Commodities to barter with the Natives. It is true that accidentally and but
very rarely a Horſe is found to help out a
little.

If they muſt venture upon the Water,
there are only ſome wretched Canoes,
made either of the Barks of Trees or of Bullocks Hides, and thoſe they muſt often
carry or drag along the Land, when the
Falls of the Rivers obſtruct making uſe of
them. All the Bed is lying on the bare
Ground, expoſed to the Inclemencies of
the Air, to be devour'd by Alligators and
bit by Rattle Snakes ; without Bread,
Wine, Salt and all other Comforts of Life,
and this for ſome Years. The Diet alto-
gether conſiſts in a poor Pap or Haſty-Pudding made of the Meal of *Indian* Corn,
Fiſh half broil'd or ill boil'd, and ſome
Beef or wild Goats Fleſh, dry'd in the Air
and Smoke. Beſides, what a Trouble is
it to invent Signs to be underſtood by ſo
many ſeveral Nations, each of which has
it's peculiar Language ? All this an Adventurer muſt reſolve with himſelf to go
through, who deſigns to make Diſcoveries
in *Canada* ; and it would be hard to believe
this

this, did not all those who write of it exactly agree in this Particular.

However that Country is good and pleasant, at least towards the South, which is what is here spoken of. The Temparature of the Climate is admirable, the Soil excellent for Tillage, and it is extraordinary fertil in all Sorts of Grain and Fruit ; which appears by those the Land produces of it self in great Plenty. The Hills and Woods produce Timber for all Uses and Fruit Trees, as well of cold as hot Countries. There are Vines which want but little Improvement ; there are Sugar-Canes, large Meadows, and navigable Rivers full of Fish. It is true they are infested with Alligators, but with a little Care they are to be avoided ; as may the Rattle-Snakes, which are extraordinary venomous, but never bite unless they are hurt. There are thousands of wild Bullocks, larger than ours, their Flesh good, and instead of Hair, they have a Sort of curl'd Wool extraordinary fine. There are Abundance of Deer, wild Goats and all Sorts of wild Fowl, and more especially of Turkeys. As there are Poisons and Venoms, so there are immediate and wonderful Antidotes.

We must not look there for rich and stately Cities, or lofty Structures, or any of those Wonders of Architecture, or the Re-

A 4

mains

mains and ancient Monuments of the Vanity of great Men ; but we may there admire Nature in its beautiful Simplicity, as it came from the Hands of its Creator ; without having been alter'd or depraved by Ambition or Art.

But is so vast and so beautiful a Country only for Beasts, Birds and Fishes! O inconceiveable Wonder! There is an infinite Number of People, divided into Nations, living in Cottages made of the Barks of Trees, or cover'd with Reeds or Hides, when they are not abroad at War, or Hunting, or Fishing, almost naked, without any other Bed but a Bullock's Hide, or any Houshold-Stuff but a Pot or Kettle, an Axe and some Platters made of Bark. They take their Sustenance, as it comes in their Way, and like the Beasts ; they have no Care, do not value Wealth, sing, dance, smoke, eat, sleep, hunt, fish ; are independant, make War, and when an Opportunity offers, take Revenge of any Injury in the most cruel Manner they are able. Such is the Life of those Savages. Tho' there be some in the Southern Parts, not quite so stupid and brutal as those in the North, yet they are both Savages, who think of Nothing but what is present, love Nothing but what is obvious to the Senses, incapable of comprehending any Thing that is Spiritual ; sharp and ingenious in

what

what is for their own Advantage, without any Sense of Honour or Humanity ; horribly cruel, perfectly united among themselves to their Nation and their Allies ; but revengeful and merciless towards their Enemies. To conclude, their Shape, tho' hideous, shews they are Men ; but their Genius and Manners render them like the worst of Beasts.

A modern Author, who has liv'd in *Canada*, and in other Respects has writ well enough, has perhas fancy'd, he might distinguish himself, and be thought more understanding than other Men in discovering the Genius of those People, by assigning more Ingenuity and Penetration to the Savages, than is generally allow'd them. He sometimes makes them to argue too strongly and too subtilely against the Mysteries of Christian Religion , and his Relation has given just Occasion to suspect, that he is himself the Libertine and Talking Savage, to whom he has given the artful Malignity of his Notions and Arguments.

La Hontan's forged Discourse with a Savage, wherein he renders himself ridiculous

As for the Genius of the Savages, I am of Opinion, we ought to believe the Missioners ; for they are not less capable than other Men to discover the Truth, and they have at least as much Probity to make it known. It is likely, that they, who have for an hundred Years past, wholly apply'd them-

themselves, according to the Duty of their Function, to study those poor Images of Men, should not be acquainted with them? Or would not their Conscience have check'd them, had they told a Lye in that Particular? Now all the Missioners agree, that allowing there are some Barbarians less wicked and brutal than the rest; yet there are none good, nor thoroughly capable of such Things as are above the Reach of our Senses; and that whatsoever they are, there is no relying on them; there is always cause to suspect them, and in short, before a Savage can be made a Christian, it is requisite to make him a Man; and we look upon those Savages as Men, who have neither King nor Law, and what is most deplorable, no God; for if we rightly examine their Sentiments and their Actions, it does not appear that they have any Sort of Religion, or well form'd Notion of a Deity. If some of them, upon certain Occasions, do sometimes own a First or Sovereign Being, or do pay some Veneration to the Sun. As to the first Article, they deliver themselves in such a confuse Manner, and with so many Contradictions and Extravagancies, that it plainly appears, they neither know nor believe anything of it; and as for the second, it is only a bare Custom, without any serious Reflection on their Part.

The Natives of Canada brutal.

A

A miferable Nation, more void of the Light of Heaven, and even that of Nature, than fo many other Nations in the *Eaft Indies,* who, tho' brutal and ftupid as to the Knowledge of the Deity, yet are not without fome Sort of Worfhip, and have their Hermits and *Fakirs* who endeavour by the Practice of horrid Penances, to gain the Favour of that Godhead, and thereby fhew they have fome real Notion of it. Nothing of that Sort is to be found among our *American* Savages, and in Conclufion, it may be faid of them in General, that they are a People without a God.

Our *French,* who are born in *Canada* all of them well fhap'd, and Men of Senfe and Worth, cannot endure to have their Savages thus run down. They affirm they are like other Men, and only want Education and being improv'd; but befides that we may believe they fay fo to fave the Honour of their Country, we advance nothing here but what is grounded on the Report of many able and worthy Perfons, who have writ of it, after being well inform'd on the Spot. We are therefore apt to believe, that there is a Diftinction to be made at prefent between two Sorts of Savages in *Canada, viz.* thofe who have been converfant among the *Europeans* for fixty or eighty Years paft, and the others who are daily difcover'd; and it is of the latter

that

that we fpeak here more particularly, and
to whom we affign all thofe odious and
wretched Qualities of the Savages of *North
America*; for it is well known, that the
firft Sort of them, as for Inftance, the *Hurons*, the *Algonquins*, the *Iroquois*, the *Iflinois* and perhaps fome others are now pretty well civiliz'd, fo that their Reafon be-
gins to clear up, and they may become capable of Inftruction.

Amazing and incomprehenfible, but at
the fame Time adorable Difpofition of Divine Providence! We fee here a vaft Tract
of the Earth, of an immenfe Extent, of a
wonderful Soil for Tillage and Fertility in
all Sorts of Fruit and Grain; of an admirable Temperature as to the Air, which
appears by the very numerous Inhabitants
being fcarce fubject to any Difeafes, and in
that theSex,which among us isweak,is there
Strong Wo- Strong and Vigorous, bringing forth their
men. Children with little or no Pain, and fuck-
ling them amidft Labour and Fatigues,
without any of thofe Miferies they are li-
able to in our Countries. Yet that vaft
and beautiful Country, defcrib'd in this
Journal, fo much favour'd with Worldly
Bleffings, has been for fo many Ages deftitute of the Heavenly.

The infinite Numbers of People inhabi-
ting it are Men, and have fcarce any thing
but the Shape; they are God's Creatures,
and

and do not so much as know, much less serve him. Those who have the Courage and Boldness to travell through the Countries of such Savages, and those who read the Relations of such Travellers, ought to take Care how they make any rash Reflections upon this Point, or pry too deeply into it; for they may chance to lose themselves in their Thoughts. The shortest and the safest Course is, in such Cases, to adore the inconceivable Profoundness of the Creator's Wisdom; to give a Check to all our Enquiries and Curiosities, with the Apostle's Exclamation, *O the Depth of the Riches both of the Wisdom and Knowledge of God! How unsearchable are his Judgments and his Ways past finding out!* And never ceasing to return Thanks to his Goodness, for having so abundantly supply'd us with his Light and Grace, to conjure him to impart the same to those poor distress'd *Americans*, and that he who is Almighty, will of those Stones make Children of *Abraham*. This all Christians are oblig'd incessantly to pray for, because as Brutish and Stupid as those Savages are, they are still our Brethren, since like us descended from *Adam* and *Noah*.

How much are we then oblig'd to those bold Travellers, who undertake new Discoveries, who to the Hazard of their Lives, at their own Expence, and with such extraordinary

traordinary Toils, go to find out for us, not only numerous Objects of our Curiosity and Admiration, which were before unknown to us, but who also discover to us a numerous Kindred, which is not ever the less such, for having been so long unknown to us. What if it be brutal and indocible, it will be the more Meritorious to Labour at Civilizing of and making it capable of receiving the Lights of Reason and of Faith. We can never sufficiently express our Gratitude to those who apply themselves to the making of new Discoveries; the more Difficulties that attend them, the more we are beholding to those who undertake them. Supposing that Avarice, Ambition, a restless Temper, or a desperate Fortune, are very often the Occasions of such Undertakings; yet God, who can draw Good out of Evil, makes all those Passions subservient to his Glory, and the Salvation of his Elect, and if long Travels do not commonly make Saints of the Travellers, it is their own Fault. However, they at least prepare the Way to the Sanctification of so many Barbarians, beating a Road for the Missioners, who go to instruct those People. Thus all the World is beholden to them; the Savages for the Knowledge of God that is procur'd them; and we for finding by their Means an infinite Number of People
before

before unknown, who will join with us in Serving and Glorifying the Creator of the Univerfe.

Granting that the faid Travellers are not fometimes exact, or agree among themfelves in their Relations, their Defcriptions and their Maps; this muft be an unavoidable Fault in Difcoverers; but even that is advantageous to the Publick, for as much as their Succeffors are excited to examine thofe Points more ftrictly, to correct, explain and afcertain thofe Miftakes.

In acknowledgment therefore of the Service done us by thofe Illuftrious Adventurers and to make them fome Sort of Amends for their Sufferings, let us tranfmit their Names to Pofterity in our Writings; let us applaud their Actions when we read them, and let us commend their Relations. This here, moft certainly deferves to be read and commended, for it is Curious, Extraordinary and Tragical. It is alfo, as has been faid before, ingaging, at this Conjuncture, when there is a Defign of making Settlements in thofe Countries, it mentions, the Confequence whereof may be moft Honourable and Advantageous to the Nation. The Travel thro' that Country is one of the greateft and moft full of Difficulties that has been perform'd; the Relation of it being made by an Eye

Witnefs

Witnefs, and in a natural, plain and particular Manner, deferves to be credited; but being only a Journal, it is not capable of admitting of Ornaments or Embellifhments. The Reader will be pleas'd to excufe the Repetition of the fame Words in it, on Account of the Impoffibility of doing otherwife, and will think it enough that the Barrennefs of the Narration is made Amends for by the Curiofity of the Subjects. I am of Opinion the fmall Notes I have added will not be difpleafing, becaufe they explain fome Particulars, which are not very intelligible to fuch as are not us'd to read many Travels.

After having faid the Good and the Bad of this *North America*, mentioning the Beauty and Excellency of its Climate and the Brutality of its People, and recited the infinite Hardfhips, thofe who defign to travel muft refolve to undergo, I am of Opinion it will be proper to fay fomething of the late Monfieur *de la Sale*, who is the principal Perfon, and as it were, the Hero of this Relation, tho' having been murdered by his own Men, he fell the unfortunate Victim of the Difcovery here treated of. It is alfo convenient to make known what went before that, which is contain'd in this Journal, and the prefent happy Confequence of that fatal Enterprize.

Here

Here follows what I have of my own particular Knowledge, and by what has been written.

Robert Cavelier, commonly call'd Monſieur *de la Sale*, a Native of *Roan*, of a good Family, having been educated in Piety and Learning, went over very young into *Canada* and took Delight in Trade, but more in Projects of new Diſcoveries up the Inland of thoſe vaſt Countries. Intending to ſettle there and make that his Country, he purchaſed an Habitation in the Iſland of *Mont-real*, where has been built the ſecond Town of *Canada*, ſixty Leagues above *Quebeck*, which is the Capital, being alſo a Biſhoprick, and the Reſidence of the Governor, the Intendant and the ſupreme Council. There are but only thoſe two Towns in the Country, beſides ſome Villages. They are both ſeated on the great River of St. *Laurence*, which coming from the S. W. is form'd or increaſed by the Waters of five prodigious freſh Water Lakes, running out one into another, and through them it paſſes to run down to diſcharge itſelf in the Ocean, at a very ſpacious Mouth, making Way for the Ships that deſign to penetrate into *Canada*.

Many Diſcoveries had been made to the Northward, before Monſieur *de la Sale*'s

Account of Monſieur de la Sale

a

Sale's Time; becaufe there being Plenty of very good Furs, the Traders of *Quebeck* and *Mont-real*, by Means of the Adventurers call'd *Wood-Men*, from their traveling thro' the Woods, had penetrated very far up the Country that Way; but none had advanc'd far towards the South or South-Weft, beyond Fort *Frontenac*, which is on the Lake *Ontario*, the neareft this Way of the five great Lakes. However, upon the Report of the Natives, it was fuppofed, that great and advantageous Difcoveries might be made. There had been much Talk of the rich Mines of St. *Barbara*, in the Kingdom of *Mexico*, and fome were tempted to give them a Vifit.

Something was known of the famous River *Miffifipi*, which it was fuppofed might fall into the South Sea, and open a Way to it. Thefe Conjectures working upon Monfieur *de la Sale*, who being zealous for the Honour of his Nation, defign'd to fignalize the *French* Name, on Account of extraordinary Difcoveries, beyond all that went before him; he form'd the Defign and refolv'd to put it in Execution. He was certainly very fit for it, and fucceeded at the Expence of his Life; for no Man has done fo much in that Way as he did for the Space of

His Character.

twenty

twenty Years he spent in that Employment. He was a Man of a regular Behaviour, of a large Soul, well enough learned, and understanding in the Mathematicks, designing, bold, undaunted, dexterous, insinuating, not to be discourag'd at any Thing, ready at extricating himself out of any Difficulties, no Way apprehensive of the greatest Fatigues, wonderful steady in Adversity, and what was of extraordinary Use, well enough versed in several Savage Languages. M. *de la Sale* having such extraordinary Talents, whereof he had given sufficient Proofs upon several Occasions, gain'd the Esteem of the Governors of *Canada*; and Messieurs *de Courcelles*, *Talon* and *de Frontenac* successively express'd the same, by often employing him in Affairs for the Honour and Advantage of the Colony.

The Government of the Fort of *Frontenac*, which is the Place farthest advanc'd among the Savages, was committed to him, and he going over into *France*, in the Year 1675, the King made him Proprietor of it, upon Condition he should put it into a better Condition than it was, which he did, as soon as return'd to *Canada*. Then came back again to *Paris*, full of the new Informations he had gain'd touching the River *Mississipi*, the Country

Is made Proprietor of Fort Frontenac.

a 2 it

runs through, the Mines, especially those of Lead and Copper, the navigable Rivers, and the Trade that might be carried on of Furs and the fine Wooll of those wild Bullocks, whereof there are infinite Numbers in the Forests. Being also furnish'd with better Accounts of that Country, than the Fables that were then publish'd, by the Name of a Voyage of the Sieur *Joliet*, he was well receiv'd at Court, and dispatch'd with the necessary Orders for proceeding on his Discoveries.

His Reputation makes Enemies. The great Reputation Monsieur *de la Sale* had gain'd, and his mighty Projects, occasion'd a Jealousy in some and Envy in others. His own Countrymen thwarted his Designs; but he surmounted all those Obstacles and return'd into *Canada*, about the Year 1678, with the Chevalier *Tonty*, an *Italian* Gentleman, a Person of Worth and that had serv'd, whom he gain'd to his Enterprize. He also pick'd up in the Country forty or fifty Persons fit for that Expedition, and among them were three Recolets, whom he carry'd over to try what might be done as to Christianity among the Savages; he was well acquainted with, and had a just Esteem for the Virtue, the Capacity and the Zeal of those good, religious Men, who

who alone firſt undertook the Miſſion into that new World, and who being ſeconded by others, have carry'd it on there, with ſo much Edification.

Monſieur *de la Sale* having ſpent two Years in going and coming, ſtill thwarted by thoſe who envy'd him in the Country, to ſuch a Degree, that had it not been for an Antidote, he muſt have dy'd of Poiſon given him by ſome Villains, could not order his Affairs and begin his Expedition till the Year 1682. He ſet out at length, and to the End his Diſcovery of the *Miſſiſipi* might be compleat, he caus'd Father *Hennepin*, a Recolet, with ſome others, to travel to the Northward, that they might find out the Source of that River, and they found it, about the 50th Degree of North Latitude. For his own Part, he proceeded to the Weſtward and found the River of the *Iſlinois*, which he call'd the River of *Seignelay*, and following its Courſe, came into the *Miſſiſipi*, where the other diſcharges it ſelf. He then concluded he had no more to do, but to run down to its Mouth, whether in the South Sea or the Gulph of *Mexico*. All along its Banks he found many Savage Nations, with whom, by Means of his Preſents, he enter'd into Alliances, and gave the

Source of the Miſſiſipi.

Iſlinois River.

Country

Country the Name of *Louisiana*, to honour the Name and Memory of our Auguft Monarch, in whofe Reign thofe
Difcoveries were made. At length, the
Courfe of the *Miffifipi* convey'd Monfieur
de la Sale to its Mouths, as falling into
the Gulph of *Mexico* in two Streams, and
he arriv'd there in the Month of *April*
1682 or 1683, for the Dates of thofe
who have writ concerning it, make either of thofe Years. He ftay'd there
fome Days, to take Obfervations and
place fome Marks which he might know
again, when he return'd. Being fatif-
fied with having found fome Part of
what he fought, he return'd the fame
Way he had gone, and came again to
Quebeck in *Canada*, in order to go over
to *France*, and thence to make a Tryal
to find that Mouth of the *Miffifipi* by
the Gulf of *Mexico*, which he had already difcover'd by the Way of *Canada*, and
to fecure it; for he thought it much more
advantageous to know it by the Way
of the Sea, than to go thither by Land,
becaufe the Voyage through *Canada* is
much longer and more troublefome,
and can be perform'd but once a Year,
whereas by the Way of the Bay of *Mexico* it is not longer, but is much more
commodious, and may be perform'd

in

PREFACE.

execute the Means for discovering the remaining Part of the World.

And in regard that the Particulars of the Discovery of those large and immense Provinces, will always be the Object of curious and understanding Persons, it is not to be wonder'd, that after what has been writ by Father Hennepin, a Recolet, the Chevalier Tonty and some others, we here now publish an Historical Journal of the last Voyage Monsieur de la Sale undertook into the Gulf of Mexico, to the Country of Louisiana, to finish what he had projected at his former Voyage, had not the Treachery of his own Men cut him off.

This Journal of Monsieur Joutel, whereof Monsieur Tonty makes mention in the Book that has been printed of the last Discoveries in America, Folio 319, has this peculiar, that it exactly contains what hapned to Monsieur de la Sale, Day by Day, in that fatal Voyage, since his Departure from Rochelle to his Death, and till the Return of his Brother Monsieur Cavelier the Priest, Monsieur Cavelier his Nephew, the Reverend Father Anastasius, the Recolet, and the said Sieur Joutel, who in Order to return to France, took that long Journey by Land, from the Gulf of Mexico to Canada, being a Tract of above 800 Leagues.

Many

PREFACE.

Many *Adventures of all Sorts, most of which are Tragical, will please the curious Reader; and above all he will admire the Protection of Divine Providence, in Conducting and Preserving that small Company throughout those vast Regions, and among so many barbarous Nations.*

We do not here pretend to Criticise upon the Work of Father Hennepin, *or that of Monsieur* Tonty; *but even their own Favourers cannot take it ill, that this Author does not sometimes say as they do; that he plainly delivers what he saw, and that he exposes to publick View all the Truths he was an Eye Witness to, without magnifying or inventing.*

It is nevertheless true, that they may be all excus'd as to some Particulars; Father Hennepin *and Monsieur* Tonty *may have seen some Things, that did not come to the Knowledge of Monsieur* Joutel; *but there is a Fact of great Consequence in the History of Monsieur* de la Sale, *which must not be pass'd over in Silence.*

It is, that Monsieur Tonty, *in his Book affirms, that Monsieur* de la Sale *at length found the Mouth of the* Missisipi, *and Monsieur* Joutel *asserts the contrary, and says, that is so far from being true, that during his last Progress towards the* Cenis, *when the said Sieur* Joutel *was with him, and*

had

PREFACE.

had never been parted, Monsieur de la Sale's principal Care was to enquire of all the Nations they pass'd through, where the Missisipi was, and could never hear any thing of it; that this is evidently made out, because if Monsieur de la Sale had found the Mouth of that River, he would infallibly have taken another Way, and other Measures, and all the Appearances are on this Side, as may be seen in this Relation.

However, this must be said in Behalf of Monsieur Tonty, that he deliver'd it upon the Report of Monsieur Cavelier the Priest, and Brother to Monsieur de la Sale; which Monsieur Cavelier might have Reasons to give out they had discover'd the Missisipi, upon the same Views as oblig'd him to conceal his Brother's Death.

Now in regard we shall see Monsieur de la Sale, for some time ranging along the Coasts of North America, to find out the Mouth of that River, it will be proper to inform those who have not seen his first Voyage, and shew them how it hapned that his Search prov'd in vain, and he was oblig'd to land in another Place.

After Monsieur de la Sale had discover'd that vast Continent, which is a Part of North America, from Canada, by the Way of Montreal, going up the River of St. Laurence, then through the Country of the
Iroquois,

PREFACE.

Iroquois, *the* Iſlinois *and others, all which he call'd* Louiſiana, *his Deſign was to find a ſhorter and a ſafer Way, than that he had Travell'd by Land.*

For this Reaſon it was, that having upon his firſt Diſcovery found the great River, call'd by the Barbarians Miſſiſipi *or* Mechaſipi, *according to Father* Hennepin, *and to which he gave the Name of* Colbert, *gueſſing by its Courſe that it fell into the Bay of* Mexico, *he reſolv'd with himſelf to find out the Mouth of it.*

In ſhort, he ran down that River, with more Danger and Toil than can be imagin'd, found it parted into two Streams and follow'd that which was moſt to the Northward, to the Place where it is loſt in the Sea. He took the Latitude that Mouth lay in, and found it was between 28 *and* 29 *Degrees North, as Monſieur* Joutel *affirms he heard him ſay. He left Marks there, return'd the ſame Way to* Canada *and thence into* France, *well pleaſed with his Diſcovery, which would have been very glorious, had he ſucceeded in his ſecond Voyage.*

But whether he did not take his Meaſures right, when he made his Obſervations aſhore, or whether that River diſgorges it ſelf at a flat Coaſt, and only leaves ſome inconſiderable Mark of its Channel for ſuch as come by Sea ; it is moſt certain, that when he

came

PREFACE.

came into the Bay of Mexico, he sought for the same Mouth in Vain, during the Space of three Weeks, and was oblig'd to go ashore to the S. W. of the Place, where it really was.

Monsieur Tonty, in his Book, Fol. 192. tells us, that he was present when Monsieur de la Sale took the Latitude of the Mouth of the Missisipi, at his first Voyage, and says it was between twenty two and twenty three Degrees North ; but that is a Mistake, which must be assigned either to the Printer, or Transcriber, for in the Map the said Monsieur Tonty has added to his Book, he places the said Mouth in about twenty six Degrees and a Half of North Latitude, and there is Reason to believe he errs in that too.

Monsieur Joutel and some others are of Opinion, that the Mouth of that Branch Monsieur de la Sale went down, is in the Bay of the Holy Ghost, and actually between the twenty eighth and twenty ninth Degrees of North Latitude, as Monsieur de la Sale found it. As for the other Channel, the same Sieur Joutel believes it is farther towards the S. W. and about the Shoals they met with about the 6th of January, 1685, between the twenty seventh and twenty eighth Degrees of North Latitude, when they were

sailing

PREFACE.

failing along the Coast of the Bay of Mexico, and that those Shoals were the Marks of a River discharging it self there, which they neglected to inquire into. If that be so, Monsieur de la Sale *was very near it, and even pass'd along before both the Mouths, but unfortunately, without perceiving them, which was the main Cause of his Death and the Ruin of his Enterprize.*

To conclude, it must be granted, that as the Return of that small Number of Persons, from a Country so remote and through so many Dangers, is a visible Effect of the Divine Protection; so it is also an Effect of Heavenly Justice to have preserv'd those Witnesses, and to have brought them Home into Monsiuer de la Sale*'s Country, to retrieve his Reputation, which had been sully'd by his Enemies.*

Monsieur de la Sale *would have been taken for a Dreamer, and even for an Impostor; his Enterprize had been condemn'd, and his Memory blasted; but God would not permit the Honour of a Man of such singular Merit to suffer; it pleas'd him to preserve and bring Home unquestionable Witnesses, who, by Word of Mouth and other undoubted Proofs of the notable Discoveries made by Monsieur* de la Sale*, have stopp'd*
the

PREFACE.

the Mouths of his Enemies, and made out the Truth of what has been asserted at the Beginning of this Discourse, viz. that Monsieur de la Sale only wanted good Fortune to secure him the Title of a great Man and a renowned Traveller.

Advertisement, *to the British Gentry.*

WHereas all Gentlemen ought to fit themselves betimes for those Employments which naturally fall to their Share, preferable to their Fellow Subjects; and that they who defign in particular to ferve their Prince Abroad, are obliged to underftand the Interefts and Pretentions of Foreign States, as well as the Laws and Conftitution of their own Country: It has been judg'd very ferviceable, by Perfons of great Experience, to have the moft celebrated Monfieur Wicquefort's Ambaffador tranflated into the Englifh Tongue, as being the only Book that perfectly exhaufts this Matter, little being written on the Subject by other Nations in Comparifon of the Italians, whofe Books are too defective and abftracted for common Practice. Propofals will fhortly be publifhed, for printing the faid Book by Subfcription, by the Undertaker Bernard Lintott between the two Temple-Gates

The Tragedy of Jane Shore, written in Shakefpear's Style, by Nicholas Row *Efq*; as it is acted at the Queen's Theatre in the Hay-Market. pr. 1 f. 6 d.

The Rape of the Lock, an heroick comical Poem, in 5 Canto's, with 6 Copper Plates, by Mr. Pope. pr. 1 s.

The Works of Monfieur de Moliere, tranflated, in 6 Vols. 12s. printed on fine Paper and new Elziver Letter.

The Clergy-man's Recreation, fhewing the Pleafure and Profit of the Art of Gard'ning. By John Lawrence. A. M. Rector of Yelvertott in Northamptonfhire, and fometime Fellow of Clare-Hall in Cambridge.

Mifcellaneous Poems and Tranflations by feveral Hands, particularly, the firft Book of Statius his Thebais tranflated. The Fable of Vertumnus and Pomoua, from the 14th Book of Ovid's Metamorphofis. To a young Lady; with the Works of Voiture. On Silence. To the Author of a Poem entituled Succeffion. The Rape of the Lock. An Ode for Mufick on St. Cecilia's Day. Windfor Foreft. To the Right *H*onourable George Ld. Lanfdown. An Effay on Criticifm. An Epigram upon Two or Three. All written by Mr. Pope.

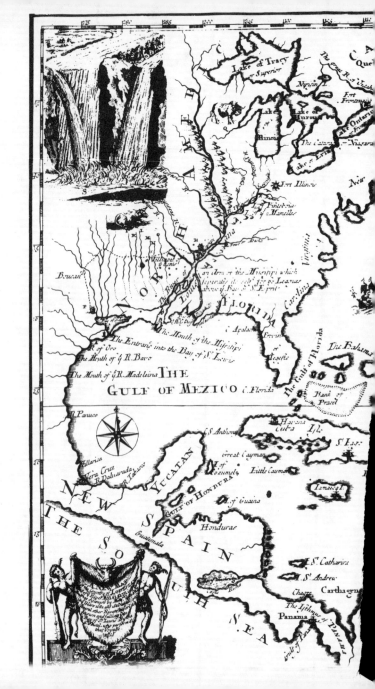

CANADA
Quebec

Lake of Tracy or Superior
Nepisin L.
Fort Frontenac
Lake Huron
Lake Ontario
The Cataract
Niagara
Illinois
Lake Erie

NORTH AMERICA

Fort Illinois

New

Fort St. Louis of the Mameltes

Brucan

Mishoure River

The River of Louisiana

an Arm of the Misisipi which separates its self for ye League above ye Bay of St. Esprit

Virginia

Carolina

FLORIDA

The Mouth of the Misisipi
R. of Oro
The Entrance into the Bay of St. Lewis
The Mouth of ye R. Bavo
The Mouth of ye R. Madeleina

Apalache Province of Tegestes

C. Florida

The Gulf of Florida

The Bahamas

THE GULF OF MEZICO

Bank of Prezel

R. Panuco

Havana
Cuba Isle
St. Iago

C. S. Anthony

Vilarica
Vera Cruz
R. Dalvarada
R. Tabasco

YUCATAN

Great Cayman
Little Cayman

I. of Cozumel

Jamaica I.

NEW SPAIN

Gulf of Honduras

I. of Guana

Honduras

Guatemala

I. St. Catharine
I. St. Andrew

THE SOUTH SEA

Costa Rica

Carthagena

Chagre
Panama
The Isthmus of Panama
Gulf of Darien

AN HISTORICAL JOURNAL

OF THE

Late Monsieur *de la Sale's*

LAST

VOYAGE

INTO

North America,

To Discover the

River *MISSISIPI.*

AT the Time when Monsieur *de la Sale* was preparing for his last Voyage into North America, I happen'd to be at Roan, the Place where he and I were both born, being return'd from the Army, where I had serv'd sixteen or seventeen Years.

It is Mr. Jourel that speaks in this Journal.

The Reputation gain'd by Monsieur *de la Sale,* the Greatness of his Undertaking, the Natural

B   Curiosity

July 1684 Curiofity which all Men are poffefs'd with,
and my Acquaintance with his Kindred, and
with feveral of the Inhabitants of that City,
who were to bear him Company, eafily prevail'd with me to make one of the Number, and
I was admitted as a Voluntier.

Our Rendezvous was appointed at *Rochel*,
where we were to imbark. Meffieurs *Cavelier*,
the one Brother, the other Nephew to Mon-
fieur *de la Sale*, Meffieurs *Chedeville*, *Planteroze*,
Thibault, *Ory*, fome others and I, repair'd thither in *July* 1684.

Departure from Ro-chel. Monfieur *de la Sale* having provided all
Things neceffary for his Voyage, furmounted all
the Difficulties laid in his Way by feveral ill-
minded Perfons, and receiv'd his Orders from
Monfieur *Arnoult*, the Intendant at *Rochel*, purfuant to thofe he had receiv'd from the King,
we fail'd on the 24th of *July*, 1684, being
twenty four Veffels, four of them for our
Voyage, and the others for the Iflands and
Canada.

Perfons that went. The four Veffels appointed for Monfieur
de la Sale's Enterprize, had on Board about
two hundred and eighty Perfons, including the
Crews; of which Number there were one hundred Soldiers, with their Officers, one *Talon*,
with his *Canada* Family, about thirty Voluntiers, fome young Women, and the reft hired
People and Workmen of all Sorts, requifite for
making of a Settlement.

Ships. The firft of the four Veffels was a Man of
War, call'd *le Joly*, of about thirty fix or forty
Guns, commanded by Monfieur *de Beaujeu*, on
which Monfieur *de la Sale*, his Brother the
Prieft, two Recolet Fryars, Meffieurs *Dain-*
maville

maville and *Chedeville*, Priests, and I imbark'd.
The next was a little Frigate, carrying six
Guns, which the King had given to Monsieur
de la Sale, commanded by two Masters; a
Flyboat of about three hundred Tuns Burden,
belonging to the Sieur *Massiot*, Merchant at
Rochel, commanded by the Sieur *Aigron*, and
laden with all the Effects Monsieur *de la Sale*
had thought necessary for his Settlement, and a
small Ketch, on which Monsieur *de la Sale* had
imbark'd thirty Tuns of Ammunition, and some
Commodities design'd for *Santo Domingo*.

All the Fleet, being under the Command of
Monsieur *de Beaujeu*, was order'd to keep together as far as *Cape Finisterre*, whence each was
to follow his own Course; but this was prevented by an unexpected Accident. We were come
into 45 Degrees 23 Minutes of North Latitude,
and about 50 Leagues from *Rochel*, when the
Boltsprit of our Ship, the *Joly*, on a sudden,
broke short, which oblig'd us to strike all our *Boltsprit*
other Sails, and cut all the Rigging the broken *lost.*
Boltsprit hung by.

Every Man reflected on this Accident according to his Inclination. Some were of Opinion it was a Contrivance; and it was debated
in Council, Whether we should proceed to *Por-*
tugal, or return to *Rochel*, or *Rochfort*; but the *Return to*
latter Resolution prevail'd. The other Ships *Rochfort.*
design'd for the Islands and *Canada*, parted from
us, and held on their Course. We made back
for the River of *Rochfort*, whither the other
three Vessels follow'd us, and a Boat was sent
in, to acquaint the Intendant with this Accident. The Boat return'd some Hours after,
towing along a Boltsprit, which was soon set in

its

its Place, and after Monsieur *de la Sale* had confer'd with the Intendant, he left that Place on the first of *August,* 1684.

We sail'd again, steering W. and by S. and on the 8th of the same Month weather'd *Cape Finisterre,* which is in 43 Degrees of North Latitude, without meeting any Thing remarkable. The 12th, we were in the Latitude of *Lisbon,* or about 39 Degrees North. The 16th, we were in 36 Degrees, the Latitude of the *Streights,* and the 20th, discover'd the Island *Madera,* which is in 32 Degrees, and where Monsieur *de Beaujeu* propos'd to Monsieur *de la Sale* to anchor, and take in Water and some Refreshments.

Cape Finisterre.

Madera.

Difference between the Commanders. Monsieur *de la Sale* was not of that Mind, on Account that we had been but twenty one Days from *France,* had sufficient Store of Water, ought to have taken aboard Refreshments enough, and it would be a Loss of eight or ten Days to no Purpose; besides, that our Enterprize requir'd Secrecy, whereas the *Spaniards* might get some Information, by Means of the People of that Island, which was not agreeable to the King's Intention.

This Answer was not acceptable to Monsieur *de Beaujeu,* or the other Officers, nor even to the Ships Crew, who mutter'd at it very much, and it went so far, that a Passenger, call'd *Paget,* a *Hugonet* of *Rochel,* had the Insolence to talk to Monsieur *de la Sale* in a very passionate and disrespectful Manner, so that he was fain to make his Complaint to Monsieur *de Beaujeu,* and to ask of him, Whether he had given any Incouragement to such a Fellow to talk to him after that Manner. Monsieur *Beaujeu* made

made him no Satisfaction. Thefe Mifunder- *Aug.*1684
ftandings,with fome others which happen'd before, being no Way advantageous to his Maje-
fty's Service, laid the Foundation of thofe tragical Events, which afterwards put an unhappy
End to Monfieur *de la Sale's* Life and Undertaking, and occafion'd our Ruin.

However, it was refolv'd not to come to an *Flying*
Anchor at that Ifland, whereupon Monfieur *de* *Fifh.*
Beaujeu faid, That fince it was fo, we fhould
put in no where but at the Ifland of *Santo Do-*
mingo. We held on our Courfe, weather'd the
Ifland of *Madera,* and began to fee thofe little
flying Fifhes, which to efcape the *Dorados,* or
Gilt-Heads, that purfue them, leap out of the
Water, take a little Flight of about a Fiftol
Shot, and then fall again into the Sea, but very
often into Ships, as they are failing by. That
Fifh is about as big as a Herring, and very
good to eat.

On the 24th, we came into the Trade Wind, *Trade*
which continually blows from Eaft to Weft,and *Wind.*
is therefore call'd by fome Authors *Ventus fub-*
*folanus,*becaufe it follows the Motion of the Sun.
The 28th,we were in 27 Degrees 44 Minutes of
North Latitude,and in 344 of Longitude. The
30th, we had a Storm, which continu'd violent
for two Days, but being right aftern of us, we
only loft Sight of the Ketch, for want of good
Steering,but fhe join'd us again a fewDays after.

The 6th of *September,*we were under the Tro-
pic of *Cancer,*in 23 Degrees 30 Minutes of North
Latitude and 319 of Longitude. There Monf. *Ducking.*
de la Sale's Obftructing the Ceremony the Sailors
call Ducking, gave them Occafion to mutter
again,and render'd himfelf privately odious. So

many have given an Account of the Nature of that Folly, that it would be needlefs to repeat it here; it may fuffice to fay, that there are three things to authorize it, 1. Cuftom. 2. The Oath adminifter'd to thofe who are duck'd, which is to this Effect, *That they will not permit any to pafs the Tropics or the Line, without obliging them to the fame Ceremony.* And 3, which is the moft prevailing Argument, the Intereft accruing to the Sailors upon that Occafion, by the Refrefhments, Liquors or Money given them by the Paffengers to be excus'd from that Ceremony.

Monfr. *de la Sale,* being inform'd that all Things were preparing for that impertinent Ceremony of Ducking, and that a Tub full of Water was ready on the Deck (*the French Duck in a great Cask of Water, the Englifh in the Sea, letting down the Perfon at the Yard Arm*) fent Word, that he would not allow fuch as were under his Command to be fubject to that Folly, which being told to Monfr. *de Beaujeu,* he forbid putting of it in Execution, to the great Diffatisfaction of the inferior Officers and Sailors, who expected a confiderable Sum of Money and Quantity of Refrefhments, or Liquors, becaufe there were many Perfons to Duck, and all the Blame was laid upon Monfr. *de la Sale.*

On the 11th of *September,* we were in the Latitude of the Ifland of *Santo Domingo,* or *Hifpaniola,* being 20 Degrees North, and the Longitude of 320 Degrees. We fteer'd our Courfe Weft, but the Wind flatting, the enfuing Calm quite ftopp'd our Way. That fame Day Monfr. *Dainmaville,* the Prieft, went aboard the Bark *la Belle,* to adminifter the Sacraments to a Gunner, who died a few Days after. Monfr: *de la*

Hifpaniola Ifland.

Sale

Sale went to see him, and I bore him Company.

The 21st, the Ketch, which we had before lost Sight of, join'd us again ; and some Complaints being made to Monsr. *de la Sale*, by several private Persons that were aboard the Flyboat, he order'd me to go thither to accomodate those Differences, which were occasion'd only by some Jealousies among them.

The 16th, we sail'd by the Island *Sombrero*, and the 18th had hard blowing Weather, which made us apprehensive of a Hurracan. The foul Weather lasted two Days, during which Time, we kept under a main Course and lost Sight of the other Vessels.

A Council was call'd aboard our Ship, the *Joly*, to consider whether we should lie by for the others, or hold on our Course, and it was resolv'd, that, considering our Water began to fall short, and there were above five Persons sick aboard, of which Number Monsr. *de la Sale* and the Surgeon were, we should make all the Sail we could, to reach the first Port of the Island *Hispaniola*, being that call'd *Port de Paix*, or Port Peace, which Resolution was accordingly register'd.

The 20th, we discover'd the first Land of *Hispaniola*, being Cape *Samana*, lying in 19 Degrees of North Latitude, and of Longitude 308. The 25th we should have put into *Port de Paix*, as had been concerted, and it was not only the most convenient Place for us to get Refreshments, but also the Residence of Monsr. *de Cussy*, Governor of the Island *Tortuga*, who knew that Monsr. *de la Sale* carried particular Orders for him to furnish such Necessaries as he stood in Need of.

Not-

Notwithſtanding theſe cogent Reaſons, Mr. *de Beaujeu* was poſitive to paſs further on in the Night, weathering the Iſland *Tortuga*, which is ſome Leagues diſtant from *Port de Paix* and the Coaſt of *Hiſpaniola.* He alſo paſs'd Cape St. *Nicolas,* and the 26th of the ſaid Month, we put into the Bay of *Jaguana,* coaſting the Iſland *Guanabo,* which is in the Middle of that great Bay or Gulph, and in Concluſion, on the 27th we arriv'd at *Petit Gouave,* having ſpent 58 Days in our Paſſage from the Port of *Chef de Bois,* near *Rochel.*

This Change of the Place for our little Squadron to put into, for which no Reaſon could be given, prov'd very diſadvantageous; and it will hereafter appear, as I have before obſerv'd, that thoſe Miſunderſtanding among the Officers infenſibly drew on the Cauſes from whence our Misfortune proceeded.

As ſoon as we had dropt Anchor, a *Piragua,* or great Sort of *Canoe,* came out from the Place, with Twenty Men, to know who we were, and hail'd us. Being inform'd that we were *French,* they acquainted us, that Monſieur *de Cuffy* was at *Port de Paix* with the Marquis *de St. Laurent,* Lieutenant General of the *American* Iſlands, and Monſieur *Begon* the Intendant, which very much troubled Monſieur *de la Sale,* as having Affairs of the utmoſt Conſequence to concert with them; but there was no Remedy, and he was oblig'd to bear it with Patience.

The next Day, being the 28th. we ſang *Te Deum,* in Thankſgiving for our proſperous Paſſage. Monſieur *de la Sale* being ſomewhat recover'd of his Indiſpoſition, went Aſhore with ſeveral of the Gentlemen of his Retinue, to buy ſome

some Refreshments for the Sick, and to find Means to send Notice of his Arrival, to Messieurs *de St. Laurent, de Cussy* and *Begon*, and signify to them, how much he was concern'd that we had not put into *Port de Paix.* He writ particularly to Monsieur *de Cussy*, to desire he would come to him, if possible, that he might be assisting to him, and take the necessary Measures for rendring his Enterprize successful, that it might prove to the King's Honour and Service.

In the mean Time, the Sick suffering very much Aboard the Ships, by Reason of the Heat, and their being too close together, the Soldiers were put Ashore, on a little Island, near *Petit Gouaves*, which is the usual Burial-Place of the People of the pretended Reformed Religion, where they had fresh Provisions, and Bread baked on Purpose, distributed to them. As for the Sick, I was order'd by Monsieur *de la Sale*, to provide a House for them, whither they were carry'd, with the Surgeons, and supply'd with all that was requisite for them.

Some Days after, Monsieur *de la Sale* fell dangerously ill, most of his Family were also sick. A violent Fever, attended with Lightheadedness, brought him almost to Extremity. The Posture of his Affairs, Want of Money, and the Weight of a mighty Enterprize, without knowing whom to trust with the Execution of it, made him still more Sick in Mind, than he was in his Body, and yet his Patience and Resolution surmounted all those Difficulties. He pitch'd upon Monsieur *le Gros* and me to act for him, caus'd some Commodities he had Aboard the Ships to be sold, to raise Money; and through our

our Care, and the excellent Conſtitution of his Body, he recover'd Health.

Whilſt he was in that Condition, two of our Ships, which had been ſeparated from us on the 18th of *September*, by the ſtormy Winds, arriv'd at *Petit Gouave* on the 2d of *October*. The Joy conceiv'd on Account of their Arrival, was much allay'd by the News they brought of the Loſs of the Ketch, taken by two *Spaniſh Piraguas* ; and that Loſs was the more grievous, becauſe that Veſſel was laden with Proviſions, Ammunition, Utenſils and proper Tools for the ſetling of our new Colonies ; a Misfortune which would not have happen'd, had Monſieur *de Beaujeu* put into *Port de Paix*, and Meſſieurs *de St. Laurent*, *de Cuſſy*, and *Begon* who arrived at the ſame Time, to ſee Monſieur *de la Sale* did not ſpare to ſignify as much to him, and to complain of that Miſcarriage.

Ketch taken by the Spaniards.

Monſieur *de la Sale* being recover'd, had ſeveral Conferences with theſe Gentlemen, relating to his Voyage. A Conſult of Pilots was called to reſolve where we ſhould touch before we came upon the Coaſt of *America*, and it was reſolved to ſteer directly for the Weſtern Point of the Iſland of *Cuba*, or for *Cape* St. *Antony*, diſtant about 300 Leagues from *Hiſpaniola*, there to expect the proper Seaſon, and a fair Wind to enter the Gulph or Bay, which is but Two hundred Leagues over.

The next Care was to lay in Store of other Proviſions, in the Room of thoſe which were loſt, and Monſieur *de la Sale* was the more preſſing for us to imbark, becauſe moſt of his Men deſerted, or were debauch'd by the Inhabitants of the Place ; and the Veſſel call'd *l' Aimable*,
being

being the worſt Sailer of our little Squadron, it was reſolv'd that ſhould carry the Light, and the others to follow it. Monſieur *de la Sale*, Monſieur *Cavelier* his Brother, the Fathers *Zenobrius* and *Anaſtaſius*, both Recolets, Monſieur *Chedeville* and I imbark'd on the ſaid *Aimable* and all ſail'd the 25th of *November*.

We met with ſome Calms, and ſome violent Winds, which neverthelefs carry'd us in Sight of the Iſland of *Cuba*, on the 30th of the ſame Month, and it then bore from us *N. W.* There we alter'd our Courſe and ſteer'd *W.* and by *N.* The 31ſt, the Weather being ſomewhat cloſe, we loſt Sight of that Iſland, then ſtood *W. N. W.* and the Sky clearing up, made an Obſervation at Noon, and found we were in 19 Degrees, 45 Minutes of North Latitude ; by which we judg'd that the Currents had carry'd us off to Sea from the Iſland of *Cuba*.

On the firſt of *December* we diſcover'd the Iſland *Cayman*. The 2d we ſteer'd *N. W.* and by *W.* in order to come up with the Iſland of *Cuba* in the Northern Latitude of 20 Degrees 32 Minutes. The 3d we diſcover'd the little Iſland of *Pines*, lying cloſe to *Cuba*. The 4th, we weather'd a Point of that Iſland, and the Wind growing ſcant, were forc'd to ply upon a Bowling, and make ſeveral Trips till the 5th at Night, when we anchor'd in a Creek, in 15 Fathom Water, and continued there till the 8th.

Cayman Iſland.

Iſland of Pines.

During that ſhort Stay, Monſieur *de la Sale* went Aſhore with ſeveral Gentlemen of his Retinue on the Iſland of *Pines*, ſhot an Alligator dead, and returning Aboard, perceiv'd he had loſt two of his Voluntiers, who had wander'd
into

into the Woods, and perhaps loſt their Way. We fired ſeveral Muſquet Shots to call them, which they did not hear, and I was order'd to expect them aſhore, with 30 Muſquetiers to attend me. They return'd the next Morning with much Trouble.

In the mean Time, our Soldiers, who had *Alligator eaten.* good Stomachs, boil'd and eat the Alligator, Monſieur *de laSale* had kill'd. The Fleſh of it was white and had a Taſte of Musk, for which Reaſon I could not eat it. One of our Hunters kill'd a wild Swine, which the Inhabitants of thoſe Iſlands call *Maron.* There are of them *Wild Swine* in the Iſland of *Santo Domingo,* or *Hiſpaniola,* they are of the Breed of thoſe the *Spaniards* left in the Iſlands when they firſt diſcover'd them, and run wild in the Woods. I ſent it to Monſieur *de la Sale*, who preſented the one Half to Monſieur *de Beaujeu.*

Iſland of That Iſland is all over very thick wooded, *Pines.* the Trees being of ſeveral Sorts, and ſome of them bear a Fruit reſembling the Acorn, but harder. There are Abundance of Parrots, larger than thoſe at *Petit Gouave,* a great Number of Turtle Doves and other Birds, and a Sort of Creatures reſembling a Rat, but as big as a Cat, their Hair reddiſh. Our Men kill'd many of them and fed heartily on them, as they did on a good Quantity of Fiſh, wherewith that Coaſt abounds.

We imbark'd again, as ſoon as the two Men who had ſtray'd were return'd, and on the 8th; being the Feaſt of the *Conception* of the Bleſſed Virgin, ſail'd in the Morning, after having heard Maſs, and the Wind ſhifting were forc'd to ſteer ſeveral Courſes. The 9th we diſcover'd

Cape

THE

PREFACE.

Written by the

Sieur *de MITCHEL*,

Who Methodiz'd this Journal.

Notwithstanding the late *Monsieur* de la Sale's *Voyage* had a most unfortunate End, as to his own Person, yet that will not hinder Posterity, from ever allowing him the Title of a most renowned Traveller.

The History of his Enterprize will be acceptable to future Ages, for laying before them, the extraordinary Genius, the invincible Courage, and the undaunted Resolution of such a Man, who could contrive and

execute

in all Seasons, either going or coming.
He was also sensible that the said Mouth
being once discover'd by Sea, afforded an
easier and safer Communication with
Canada, running up that noble River,
the Navigation whereof is not interrupted by Falls, nor Torrents for above
sixty Leagues towards its Source.

These Considerations mov'd Monsieur
de la Sale to take another Voyage into
France, where his Expedition having
been commended and his new Project
approv'd of, the King order'd him Vessels to return and carry on his Enterprize, the Particulars whereof are to
be found in this Journal. That Affair,
so well begun, seem'd to promise very
advantageous Consequences; but it mis-
carried through the Perfidiousness and
Villany of that noble Adventurer's own
People.

This is what I have judg'd might
serve as an Introduction to your Journal, if it shall not be thought to disho-
nour it, you may place it before the said
Journal, and that which follows at the
End of it, which will shew how far that
great Enterprize of the Discovery of the
Missisipi has been carried.

The other Part here mention'd is at the End of the Journal.

THE

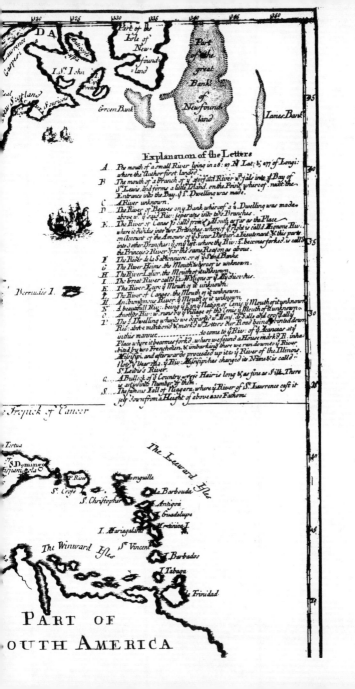

DA

Part of the Isle of New foundland

I. St. Ihn

Green Bank

Part of the great Bank of Newfoundland

James Bank

Bermudes I.

Explanation of the Letters

A. The mouth of a small River lying in 28: 27 N Lat: & 277 of Longi: where the Author first landed.

B. The mouth of a Branch of ye aforesaid River wch falls into ye Bay of St Lewis, and forme a little Island, on the Point whereof, next the Entrance unto the Bay, ye Dwelling was made.

C. A River unknown.

D. The River of Beeves on ye Bank whereof a ye Dwelling was made, above wch ye said Riv: seperates into two Branches.

E. The River of Canse so called from ye Mouth, as far as the Place where it divides into two Branches, whereof ye right is call'd Magnone Riv: on Account of the Amours of ye Sieur Darbut a Lieutenant & this parts into 2 other Branches: ye one left, where the Riv: S becomes forked, is call'd the Princess's River for the same Reason as above.

F. The River de la St Pennieur, or of ye Sand Banks.

G. The River Beime, the Mouth whereof is unknown.

H. The River Lalier, the Mouth of it unknown.

I. The great River call'd Vu Msigne or of Mychisichu.

K. The River Eure, ye Mouth of it unknown.

L. The River of Canser, the Mouth of it unknown.

M. An Anonymous River ye Mouth of it unknown.

N. A beautiful Riv: being ye of ye Tenic ye Mouth of it unknown.

O. Another Riv: wch runs by ye Village of the Tenic wch falls and crosses ally.

P. The S Dwelling whence we departed wth Mons: de Salle, and proceeded down Riv: above mentioned & mark'd wth Letters. Her Road being represented down in this manner............to come to ye Riv: of ye Akancas at ye Place where it becomes forked, where we found a House inhabited by two Frenchmen, & imbarking there we ran down to ye River Mississipi, and afterwards proceeded up its ye River of the Illinois. Note ye Year that ye Riv: Mississipi has changed its Name & is call'd St Lewis's River.

R. A Bullock of ye Country whose Hair is long & as fine as Silk. There is infinite Number of them.

S. The famous Fall of Niagara, where ye River of St Lawrence casts itself down from a Height of above 2200 Fathom.

Tropick of Cancer

Tortua
S Domingo
P. Rico
S. Croix
S. Christopher
Longuille
La Barbouda
Antigoa
Guadelupe
I. Mariagalante
Martinico I.
The Leeward Isles
St Vincent
Barbados
I Tabaga
Trinidad
The Winward Isles

PART OF

SOUTH AMERICA

Cape *Corrientes,* of the Island of *Cuba*; where we were first becalm'd; and then follow'd a stormy Wind, which carried us away five Leagues to the Eastward. The 10th we spent the Night, making several Trips. The 11th, the Wind coming about, we weather'd Cape *Corrientes,* to make that of St. *Antony*; and at length, after plying a considerable Time, and sounding, we came to an Anchor the 12th, upon good Ground, in fifteen Fathom Water, in the Creek form'd by that Cape, which is in 22 Degrees of North Latitude and 288 Degrees 35 Minutes of Longitude.

We stay'd there only till next Day, being the 13th, when the Wind seem'd to be favourable to enter upon the Bay of *Mexico.* We made ready and sail'd, steering *N. W.* and by *N.* and *N. N. W.* to weather the said Cape and prosecute our Voyage: But by that Time we were five Leagues from the Place of our Departure, we perceiv'd the Wind shifted upon us, and not knowing which Way the Currents sate, we stood *E.* and by *N.* and held that Course till the 14th, when Monsieur *de Beaujeu,* who was aboard the *Joly,* join'd us again, and having confer'd with Monsieur *de la Sale* about the Wind's being contrary, propos'd to him to return to Cape St. *Antony,* to which Monsieur *de la Sale* consented, to avoid giving him any Cause to complain, tho' there was no great Occasion for so doing, and accordingly we went and anchor'd in the Place from whence we came.

The next Day, being the 15th, Monsieur *de la Sale* sent some Men ashore, to try whether we could fill some Casks with Water. They brought Word, they had found some in the
Wood,

Wood, which was not much amifs, but that there was no Conveniency for rowling of the Casks ; for which Reafon Rundlets were fent, and as much Water brought in them, as fill'd fix or feven of our Water Casks.

The fame Men reported, that they had found a glafs Bottle, and in it a little Wine, or fome other Liquor, almoft dead. This was all the Provifion we found in that Place, by which it *Miftake in* appears, how much Monfieur *Tonti* was mifin-*Monfieur* form'd, fince in his Book, *Pag.* 242, he fays, *Tonti's* we found in that Ifland feveral Tun of *Spanifh* *Account of* Wine, good Brandy and *Indian* Wheat, which *thisVoyage.* the *Spaniards* had left or abandon'd ; and it is a meer Invention without any Thing of Truth.

The 16th, the Weather being ftill Calm, the Men went afhore again for five or fix more Casks of Water. I was to have gone with them, had not an Indifpofition, which I firft felt in the Ifland of *Pines,* and afterwards turn'd to a tertian Ague, prevented me. Therefore I can give no Account of that Ifland, any further than what I could fee from the Ships, which was Abundance of that Sort of Palm-Trees, in French call'd *Lataniers,* fit for nothing but making of Brooms, or fcarce any other Ufe. That Day we faw fome Smoaks, far within the Ifland, and guefs'd they might be a Signal of the Number of our Ships, or elfe made by fome of the Country Hunters, who had loft their Way.

The next Night preceding the 17th, the Wind frefhning from the *N. W.* and ftarting up all on a fudden, drove the Veffel call'd *la Belle* upon her Anchor, fo that fhe came foul of the Boltfprit of the *Aimable,* carrying away the
Sprit-

Spritfail-Yard and the Spritfail-Top-Sail-Yard, and had not they immediately veer'd out the Cable of the *Aimable*, the Veffel *la Belle* would have been in danger of perifhing, but efcap'd with the Lofs of her Mizen, which came by the Board, and of about a hundred Fathoms of Cable and an Anchor.

The 18th, the Wind being frefh, we made ready, and fail'd about Ten in the Morning, ftanding *North* and *N.* and by *W.* and held our Courfe till Noon; the Point of Cape St. *Anthony* bearing *Eaft* and *Weft* with us, and fo continu'd fteering *North-Weft*, till the 19th at Noon, when we found our felves in the Latitude of 22 Degrees 58 Minutes *North*, and in 287 Degrees 54 Minutes Longitude.

Finding the Wind fhifting from one Side to another, we directed our Courfe feveral Ways, but that which prov'd advantageous to us, was the fair Weather, and that was a great Help, fo that fcarce a Day pafs'd without taking an Obfervation.

The 20th, we found the Variation of the Needle was 5 Degrees *Weft*, and we were in 26 Degrees 40 Minutes of North Latitude and 285 Degrees 16 Minutes Longitude. The 23th it grew very cloudy, which threaten'd ftormy Weather, and we prepar'd to receive it, but came off only with the Apprehenfion, the Clouds difperfing feveral Ways, and we continu'd till the 27th in and about 28 Degrees 14 Minutes, and both by the Latitude and Eftimation it was judg'd, that we were not far from Land.

The Bark call'd *la Belle* was fent out to difcover and keep before, founding all the Way; and half an Hour before Sun-fet, we faw the

Veffel

Veffel *la Belle* put out her Colours and lie by for us. Being come up with her, the Mafter told us, he had found an Owzy Bottom at thirty two Fathom Water. At eight of the Clock we founded alfo, and found forty Fathom, and at ten, but twenty five. About Midnight, *la Belle* founding again, found only feventeen, which being a Demonftration of the Nearnefs of the Land, we lay by for the *Joly*, to know what Monfieur *de Beaujeu* defign'd, who being come up, lay by with us.

The 27th, Monfieur *de Beaujeu* fent the *Chevalier d'Aire*, his Lieutenant, and two Pilots to Monfieur *de la Sale*, to conclude upon the Courfe we were to fteer, and it was agreed we fhould ftand Weft North Weft till we came into fix Fathom Water ; that then we fhould run Weft, and when we had difcover'd the Land, Boats fhould be fent to view the Country. Matters being thus agreed on, we fail'd again, founding all the Way for the more Security, and about ten, were in ten or eleven Fathom Water, the Bottom fine greyifh Sand and owzy. At Noon, were in 26 Degrees 37 Minutes of North Latitude.

The 28th, being in eight or nine Fathom Water, we perceiv'd the Bark *la Belle*, which kept a Head of us, put out her Colours, which was the Signal of her having difcover'd Something. A Sailor was fent up to the Main-Top, who defcry'd the Land, to the N. E. not above fix Leagues Diftance from us, which being told to Monfieur *de Beanjeu*, he thought fit to come to an Anchor.

There being no Man among us who had any Knowledge of that Bay, where we had been told

told the Currents were ſtrong, and ſate ſwiftly *Dec.1684* to the *Eaſtward*, it made us ſuſpect that we were fallen off, and that the Land we ſaw muſt be the Bay of *Apalache*, which oblig'd us on the 29th to ſteer *W. N. W.* ſtill keeping along the Land, and it was agreed that the *Joly* ſhould follow us in ſix Fathom Water.

The 30th, the *Chevalier d' Aire* and the ſecond Pilot of the *Joly* came aboard us to confer and adjuſt by our Recknings what Place we might be in, and they all agreed, according to Monſieur *de la Sale*'s Opinion, that the Cur- *Currents.* rents had ſet us to the *Eaſtward*, for which Reaſon we held on our Courſe, as we had done the Day before to the *N. W.* keeping along the Shore till the firſt of *January* 1685. when we perceiv'd that the Currents forc'd us towards the Land, which oblig'd us to come to an Anchor in ſix Fathom Water.

We had not been there long, before the Bark *la Belle* made a Signal that ſhe had diſcover'd Land, which we deſcry'd at about 4 Leagues Diſtance from us. Notice was given to Monſieur *de Beaujeu*, who drew near to us, and it was reſolv'd to ſend ſome Perſon to diſcover and take an Account of the Land that appear'd to us.

Accordingly a Boat was man'd, and into it went Monſieur *de la Sale*, the *Chevalier de Aire* and ſeveral others; another Boat was alſo put out, aboard which I went with Ten or Twelve of our Gentlemen, to join Monſieur *de la Sale* and the Bark *la Belle* was order'd to follow always keeping along the Shore; to the End that if the Wind ſhou'd riſe, we might get aboard her, to loſe no Time.

C   Some

Jan. 1685

First Landing.

Some of those who were in Monsieur *de la Sale*'s Boat, and the foremost, went ashore and saw a spacious plain Country of much Pasture Ground ; but had not the Leisure to make any particular Discovery, because the Wind freshning, they were oblig'd to return to their Boat, to come aboard again ; which was the Reason why we did not go quite up to the Shore, but return'd with them to our Ship. All that could be taken Notice of was a great Quantity of Wood along the Coast. We took an Observation and found 29 Degrees 10 Minutes of North Latitude.

The Second, there arose a Fog, which made us lose Sight of the *Joly.* The next Day, the Weather clearing up, we fir'd some Cannonshot and the *Joly* answer'd, and towards the Evening we perceiv'd her to the Windward of us. We held on our Course, making several Trips till the Fourth in the Evening, when being in Sight and within two Leagues of the Land, we came to an Anchor to expect the *Joly,* for which we were in Pain.

Monsieur Joutel believes here was one of the Mouths of the Mississipi. See the Pref. and what follows.

The Fifth, we set Sail and held on our Course *W. S. W.* keeping along the Shore till about Six in the Evening, when we stood away to the Southward and anchor'd at Night in six Fathom Water. The Sixth, we would have made ready to sail, but the Pilot perceiving, that the Sea broke astern of us, and that there were some Shoals, it was thought proper to continue at Anchor, till the Wind chang'd, and we accordingly staid there the Sixth and all the Seventh. The Eighth the Wind veering about, we stood out a little to Sea, to avoid those Shoals, which are very dangerous, and anchor'd again a League
from

from thence. Upon Advice, that the Bark *la Belle* had discover'd a small Island, which appear'd between the two Points of a Bay, Monsieur *de la Sale* sent a Man up to the round Top, from whence both the one and the other were plainly to be seen, and according to the Sea Charts we had with us, that was suppos'd to be the Bay of the *Holy Ghost*.

The Ninth, Monsieur *de la Sale*, sent to view those Shoals. Those who went reported there was a sort of Bank, which runs along the Coast; that they had been in one Fathom Water and discover'd the little Island before-mention'd, and as for the Sand Bank there is no such thing mark'd down in the Charts. Monsieur *de la Sale* having examin'd the Recknings, was confirm'd in his Opinion, that we were in the Bay of *Apalache*, and caus'd us to continue the same Course.

The Tenth, he took an Observation and found 29 Degrees 23 Minutes North Latitude. The eleventh, we were becalm'd, and Monsieur *de la Sale* resolv'd to go ashore, to endeavour to discover what he was looking for; but as we were making ready, the Pilot began to mutter because five or six of us were going with Monsieur *de la Sale*, who too lightly alter'd his Design, to avoid giving Offence to brutish People. In that Particular he committed an irretrieveable Error; for it is the Opinion of Judicious Men, who, as well as I, saw the rest of that Voyage, that the Mouth of one of the Branches of the *Missisipi* River, and the same whose Latitude Monsieur *de la Sale* had taken, when he travell'd to it from *Canada*, was not far from

that

that Place, and that we muſt of Neceſſity be near the Bay of the *Holy Ghoſt.*

It was Monſieur *de la Sale*'s Deſign to find that Bay, and having found it, he had reſolv'd to have ſet aſhore about thirty Men, who were to have follow'd the Coaſt on the Right and Left, which would infallibly have diſcover'd to him that fatal River, and have prevented many Misfortunes ; but Heaven refus'd him that Succeſs, and even made him regardleſs of an Affair of ſuch Conſequence, ſince he was ſatisfy'd with ſending thither the Pilot, with one of the Maſters of the Bark *la Belle,* who return'd without having ſeen any Thing, becauſe a Fog happen'd to riſe , only the Maſter of the Bark ſaid he believ'd there was a River oppoſite to thoſe Shoals, which was very likely, and yet Monſieur *de la Sale* took no Notice of it, nor made any Account of that Report.

The Twelfth, the Wind being come about we weigh'd and directed our Courſe *S. W.* to get further from the Land. By an Obſervation found 25 Degrees 50 Minutes North Latitude, and the Wind ſhifting, and the Currents, which ſet from the Seaward driving us aſhore, it was found convenient to anchor in four or five Fathom Water, where we ſpent all the Night.

The Thirteenth, we perceiv'd our Water began to fall ſhort, and therefore it was requiſite to go aſhore to fill ſome Casks. Monſieur *de la Sale* propos'd it to me to go and ſee it perform'd, which I accepted of, with ſix of our Gentlemen who offer'd their Service. We went into the Boat, with our Arms, the Boat belonging to the Bark *la Belle* follow'd ours, with

with five or six Men, and we all made directly for the Land.

We were very near the Shoar, when we difcover'd a Number of naked Men marching along the Banks, whom we fuppos'd to be native Savages. We drew within two Musket Shots of the Land, and the Shore being flat, the Wind fetting from the Offing, and the Sea running high, dropt our Anchors, for Fear of ftaving our Boats.

When the Savages perceiv'd we had ftopp'd, they made Signs to us with Skins, to go to them, fhew'd us their Bows, which they laid down upon the Ground, and drew near to the Edge of the Shore; but becaufe we could not get Afhore, and ftill they continued their Signals, I put my Handkerchief on the End of my Firelock, after the Manner of a Flag, and made Signs to them to come to us. They were fome Time confidering of it, and at laft fome of them ran into the Water up to their Shoulders, till perceiving that the Waves overwhelm'd them, they went out again, fetch'd a large Piece of Timber, which they threw into the Sea, plac'd themfelves along both Sides of it, holding faft to it with one Arm, and fwiming with the other; and in that Manner they drew near to our Boat.

Savages came to the Boat.

Being in Hopes that Monfr. *de la Sale*, might get fome Information from thofe Savages, we made no Difficulty of taking them into our Boat, one after another, on each Side, to the Number of five, and then made Signs to the reft to go to the other Boat, which they did, and we carry'd them on Board.

Carryed Aboard.

C 3

Mon-

 Monfieur *de la Sale* was very well pleas'd to
see them, imagining they might give him fome
Account of the River he fought after; but to no
Purpofe, for he fpoke to them in feveral of the
Languages of the Savages, which he knew, and
made many Signs to them, but ftill they underftood not what he meant, or if they did comprehend any thing, they made Signs, that they
knew nothing of what he ask'd ; fo that having
made them fmoak and eat, we fhewed them
our Arms and the Ship, and when they faw at
one End of it fome Sheep, Swine, Hens and
Turkeys, and the Hide of a Cow we had kill'd,
they made Signs that they had of all thofe Sorts
of Creatures among them.

 We gave them fome Knives and Strings of
Beads, after which, they were difmifs'd, and
the Waves hindring us from coming too near
the Shore, they were oblig'd to leap into the
the Water, after we had made faft about their
Necks, or to the Tuft of Hair they have on
the Top of the Head, the Knives and other
fmall Prefents Monfieur *de la Sale* had given
them.

They went and join'd the others who expected
them, and were making Signs to us to go to
them ; but not being able to make the Shore,
we ftood off again and return'd to our Ship.
It is to be obferved, that when we were carrying
them back, they made fome Signs to us, by
which we conceiv'd they would fignify to us
that there was a great River that Way we
were pafs'd, and that it occafion'd the Shoals
we had feen.

The

The Wind changing, the same Day, we *Jan.* 1685 weigh'd Anchor and stood to the Southward, to get into the Offing, till the 14th in the Morning, when we were becalm'd. At Noon, we were in 28 Degrees 51 Minutes of North Latitude. The Wind freshned, and in the Evening we held on our Course, but only for a short Time, because the Wind setting us towards the Shore, we were obliged to anchor again, whereupon Monsieur *de la Sale* again resolved to send Ashore, and the same Persons imbark'd in the same Boats to that Effect.

We met with the same Obstacles, that had hinder'd us the Day before, that is, the High-Sea, which would not permit us to come near the Shore, and were obliged to drop Anchor in fourteen Foot Water. The Sight of Abundance of Goats and Bullocks, differing in Shape, from ours, and running along the Coast, heighten'd our Earnestness to be Ashore. We therefore founded to see whether we might get to Land by Stripping, and found we were on a Flat, which had four Foot Water, but that beyond it there was a deep Channel. Whilst we were consulting what to do, a Storm arose, which oblig'd Monsieur *de la Sale* to fire a Gun for us to return Aboard, which we did against our Inclination.

Goats and Bullocks.

Monsieur *de la Sale* was pleas'd with the Report we made him, and by it, several were encouraged to go Ashore to hunt, that we might have some fresh Meat. We spent all that Night, till the next Morning, in Hopes of returning soon to that Place; but the Wind changing, forc'd us to weigh and sail till the Evening, when we drop'd Anchor in six Fathom Water.

C 4

The

Jan. 1685 The Land which we never departed from very
far, appear'd to us very pleafant, and having
lain there till the 16th, that Morning we fail'd
W. S. W. We weather'd a Point, keeping a large
Offing, becaufe of the Sea's beating upon it,
and ftood to the Southward. At Noon, we
were in 28 Degrees 20 Minutes of North Latitude, and confequently found the Latitude declin'd, by which we were fenfible, that the
Coaft tendred to the Southward. At Night we
anchor'd in fix Fathom Water.

The 17th, the Wind continuing the fame,
we held on our Courfe *S. W.* and having
about Ten difcover' a Sort of River, Monfieur
de la Sale caus'd Ten of us to go into a Boat,
to take a View of that Coaft, and fee whether
there was not fome Place to land. He order'd
me, in Cafe we fouud any convenient Place, to
give him Notice either by Fire or Smoke.

We fet out, and found the Shoals obftructed
our Defcent. One of our Men went naked into
Second the Water to found that Sand Bank, which lay
landing. between us and the Land ; and having fhewn
us a Place where we might Pafs, we, with much
Difficulty, forc'd our Boat into the Channel,
and fix or feven of us landed, after ordering the
Boat to go up into that which had appeared to
us to be a River, to fee whether any frefh Water could be found.

As foon as we were landed, I made a Smoke
to give Notice to Monfieur *de la Sale*, and then
we advanc'd both Ways, without ftragling too
far, that we might be ready to receive Monfr.
de la Sale, who was to come, as he did, foon
after, but finding the Surges run high, he return'd

turn'd, and our Boat finding no fresh Water, *Jan.* 1685 came back and anchor'd to wait for us.

We walked about every Way, and found a dry Soil, tho' it seem'd to be overflow'd at some Times; great Lakes of salt Water, little Grass, the Track of Goats, on the Sand, and saw Herds of them, but could not come near them, however we kill'd some Ducks and Bustards. In the Evening, as we were returning, we miss'd an English Seaman, fir'd several Shot to give him Notice, searched all about, waited till after Sunset, and at last hearing no Tidings of him, we went into the Boat to return Aboard.

I gave Monsieur *de la Sale* an Account of what we had seen, which would have pleas'd him, had the River we discover'd, afforded fresh Water: He was also uneasy for the lost Man; but about Midnight we saw a Fire Ashore, in the Place we came from, which we supos'd to be made by our Man, and the Boat went for him as soon as soon as it was Day on the 18th.

After that, we made several Trips, still steering towards the *S. W.* and then ensued a Calm, which oblig'd us to come to an Anchor. Want of Water made us think of returning towards the River, where we had been the Day before. Monsr. *de la Sale* resolved to set a considerable Number of Men Ashore, with sufficient Ammunition, and to go with them himself, to discover and take Cognizance of that Country, and order'd me to follow him. Accordingly we sail'd back, and came to an Anchor in the same Place.

All Things necessary for that End being order'd on the 19th, Part of the Men were put into a Boat; but a very thick Fog rising, and taking

taking away the Sight of Land, the Compass was made use of, and the Fog dispersing as we drew near the Land, we perceiv'd a Ship making directly towards us, and that it was the *Joly*, where Monsr. *de Beaujeu* commanded, which rejoic'd us, but our Satisfaction was not lasting, and it will appear by the Sequel, that it were to have been wished, that Monsieur *de Beaujeu* had not joyn'd us again, but that he had rather gone away for *France*, without ever seeing of us.

His Arrival disconcerted the Execution of our Enterprize. Monsr. *de la Sale*, who was already on his Way, and those who were gone before him, return'd Aboard, and some Hours after, Monsr. *de Beaujeu* sent his Lieutenant, Monsr. *de Aire*, attended by several Persons, as well Clergymen as others, among whom was the Sieur *Gabaret*, second Pilot of the *Joly*.

Commanders at Variance. Monsieur *d' Aire* complain'd grievously to Monsieur *de la Sale*, in the Name of Monsr. *de Beaujeu*, for that said he, we had left him designedly; which was not true, for as I have said, the *Joly* lay at Anchor A-head of us, when we were separated from her; we fired a Gun to give her Notice of our Departure, as had been concerted, and Monsr. *de Beaujeu* answer'd it; besides that, if we had intended to separate from him, we should not have always held our Course in Sight of Land, as we had done, and that had Monsieur *de Beaujeu* held the same same Course, as had been agreed, he had not been separated from us.

There were afterwards several Disputes between the Captains and the Pilots, as well Aboard Monsieur *de la Sale*, as Aboard Monsieur

de

de Beajeu, when those Gentlemen return'd, a-
bout settling exactly the Place we were in, and
the Course we were to steer ; some positively
affirming we were farther than we imagin'd, and
that the Currents had carry'd us away ; and
others, that we were near the *Magdalen* River.

The former of those Notions prevail'd,   *They pass*
whence, upon Reflection, Monsieur *de la Sale*   *the Mouth*
concluded, that he must be past his River,   *of the* Mis-
which was but too true ; for that River empty-   *tisipi.*
ing it self in the Sea by two Channels, it follow'd that one of the Mouths fell about the
Shoals we had observ'd the sixth of the Month ;
and the rather because those Shoals were very
near the Latitude that Monsieur *de la Sale* had
observ'd, when he came by the Way of *Canada* to discover the Mouth of that River, as he
told me several Times.

This Consideration prevail'd with Monsieur
de la Sale to propose his Design of returning towards those Shoals. He gave his Reasons for
so doing and expos'd his Doubts ; but his ill
Fortune made him not be regarded. Our Pas-
sage had taken up more Time than had been expected, by Reason of the Calms ; there was a
considerable Number of Men aboard the *Joly,*
and Provisions grew short, insomuch that they
said it would not hold out to return, if our Departure were delay'd. For this Reason Monsieur *de Beaujeu* demanded Provisions of Monsieur *de la Sale* ; but he asking enough for a long
Time, Monsieur *de la Sale* answer'd, he could
only give him enough for a Fortnight, which
was more Time than was requisite to reach the
Place he intended to return to ; and that besides
he

Jan. 1685 he could not give him more Provifions, without rummaging all the Stores to the Bottom of the Hold, which would endanger his being caft away. Thus nothing was concluded, and Monfieur *de Beaujeu* return'd to his own Ship.

Third Landing. In the mean Time, Want of Water began to pinch us, and Monfieur *de la Sale* refolv'd to fend to look for fome about the next River. Accordingly he order'd the two Boats that had been made ready the Day before, to go off. He was aboard one of them himfelf, and directed me to follow him. Monfieur *de Beaujeu* alfo commanded his Boat to go for Wood. By the Way we met the faid Sieur *de Beaujeu* in his Yaul, returning from Land, with the Sieur *Minet,* an Ingenier, who told us, they had been in a Sort of falt Pool, two or three Leagues from the Place where the Ships were at Anchor, we held on our Way and landed.

One of our Boats, which was gone ahead of us, had been a League and a half up the River, without finding any frefh Water in its Channel; but fome Men wandering about to the right and left, had met with divers Rivulets of very good Water, wherewith many Casks were fill'd.

We lay afhore, and our Hunters having that Day kill'd good Store of Ducks, Buftards and Teal, and the next Day two Goats, Monfieur *de la Sale* fent Monfieur *de Beaujeu* Part. We feafted upon the reft, and that good Sport put feveral Gentlemen that were then aboard Monfieur *de Beaujeu,* among whom were Monfieur *du Hamel,* the Enfign and the King's Clerk, upon coming afhore to partake of the Diverfion; but they took much Pains and were no fuccefsfull in their Sport. I

In the mean Time many Casks were fill'd with Water, as well for our Ship as for Monſieur *de Beaujeu*'s. Some Days after Monſieur *d' Aire* the Lieutenant, came aſhore to confer with Monſieur *de la Sale*, and to know how he would manage about the Proviſions; but both of them perſiſting in their firſt Propoſals and Monſieur *de la Sale* perceiving that Monſieur *de Beaujeu* would not be ſatisfied with Proviſions for 15 Days, which he thought ſufficient to go to the Place where he expected to find one of the Branches of the *Miſſiſipi*, which he with good Reaſon believ'd to be about the Shoals, I have before ſpoken of, nothing was concluded as to that Affair. Monſieur *d' Aire* return'd to his Captain, and Monſieur *de la Sale* reſolv'd to land his Men; which could not be done for ſome Days, becauſe of the foul Weather; but in the mean Time we kill'd much Game.

During this little Interval, Monſieur *de la Sale* being impatient to get ſome Intelligence of what he ſought after, reſolv'd to go himſelf upon Diſcovery, and to ſeek out ſome more uſeful and commodious River than that where they were. To this Purpoſe he took five or ſix of us along with him. We ſet out one Morning in ſo thick a Fog, that the hindmoſt could not perceive the Track of the foremoſt, ſo that we loſt Monſieur *de la Sale* for ſome Time.

We travel'd till about three in the Afternoon, finding the Country for the moſt Part Sandy, little Graſs, no freſh Water, unleſs in ſome Sloughs, the Track of abundance of wild Goats, Lakes full of Ducks, Teals, Water-Hens, and having taken much Pains return'd without Suc-

The

The next Morning, Monfieur *de la Sale's In-dian*, going about to find wild Goats, came to a Lake, which had a little Ice upon it, the Weather being cold, and Abundance of Fifh dying about the Edges of it. He came to inform us, we went to make our Provifion of them, there were fome of a prodigious Magnitude, and among the reft extraordinary large Trouts. or elfe they were fome Sort of Fifh very like them. We caufed fome of each of a Sort to be boil'd in falt Water, and found them very good. Thus having Plenty of Fifh and Flefh, we began to ufe ourfelves to eat them both, without Bread.

Whilft we liv'd thus eafy enough, Monfieur *de la Sale* expected with Impatience to know what Refolution Monfieur *de Beaujeu* would take ; that he might either go to the Place, where he expected to find the *Miffifipi*, or follow fome other Courfe ; but at laft, perceiving that his Affairs did not advance, he refolv'd to put his own Defign in Execution, the Purport whereof was to land one hundred and twenty, or one hundred and thirty Men to go along the Coaft and continue it, till they had found fome other River, and that at the fame Time the Bark *la Belle* fhould hold the fame Courfe at Sea, ftill keeping along the Coaft, to relieve thofe Afhore in Time of Need.

He gave me and Monfieur *Moranget*, his Nephew, the Command of that fmall Company, he furnifh'd us with all Sorts of Provifion for eight, or ten Days, as alfo Arms, Tools and Utenfils we might have Occafion for, of which every Man made his Bundle. He alfo gave written Inftructions of what we were to do,

Sig

Signals we were to make; and thus we set out on the Fourth of *February*.

We took our Way along the Shore. Our firſt Day's Journey was not long, we encamp'd on a little riſing Ground, heard a Cannon ſhot, which made us uneaſy, made the Signals that had been appointed, and the next Day, being the 5th, we held on our March, Monſieur *Moranget* bringing up the Rear, and I leading the Van.

I will not ſpend Time in relating ſeveral perſonal Accidents, inconſiderable in themſelves, or of no Conſequence, the moſt conſiderable of them being the Want of freſh Water ; but will procced to ſay, that after three Days March we found a great River, where we halted and made the Signals agreed on, encamping on a commodious Spot of Ground till we could hear of the Boat, which was to follow us, or of our Ships.

But our Proviſions beginning to fall ſhort, and none of our Ships appearing, being beſides apprehenſive of ſome unlucky Accident occaſion'd by the Diſagreement between Monſieur *de la Sale* and Monſr. *de Beaujeu*, the Chief of our Company came together to know what Reſolution we ſhould take. It was agreed, that we ſhould ſpare our Proviſions to endeavour to go on to ſome Place where we might find Bullocks ; but it was requiſite to croſs the River, and we knew not how, becauſe we were too many of us, and therefore it was decreed to ſet ſome Carpenters there were among us at Work to build a little Boat, which took them up the eleventh and twelfth of *February*.

The

The 13th, we were put out of our Pain by two Veffels we difcover'd at Sea, which we knew to be the *Joly* and *la Belle*, to whom we made our Signals with Smoke. They came not in then, becaufe it was late, but the next Day being the 14th in the Morning, the Boat, with the Sieur *Barbier* and the Pilot of the Bark *la Belle* come up, and both founded the Mouth of the River.

A fine River.

They found on the Bar, from ten to twelve Foot Water, and within it from five to fix Fathom ; the Breadth of the River being about half a Quarter of a League. They founded near the Ifland, which lies between the two Points of the Bay, and found the fame Depth. The Boat of the *Joly* came and founded on the other Side of the Channel, and particularly along the Shoals, I know not to what Purpofe. The fame Day, Monfieur *de la Sale*, for whom we were much in Pain, came alfo, and as foon as he arrived, he caus'd the Boat to be laden with fuch Provifions as we ftood in Need of, but the Wind being contrary, it could not come to us till the next Day, being the 15th.

That fame Day, Monfr. *de la Sale* came Afhoar to view the Place and examine the Entrance into the River, which he found to be very good. Having confider'd all Particulars, he refolv'd to fend in the Bark *la Belle* and l' *Aimable*, that they might be under Shelter, to which Purpofe, he order'd to found, and to know whether thofe two Veffels could both come in that fame Day. Monfieur *de Beaujeu* caus'd alfo the Place to be founded, and lay Afhoar on the other Side of the River, where he took Notice there were Vines which run up the Trees, like

our

our Wall Vines, fome Woods and the Carcaffes of Bullocks, which he fuppofed to have died with Thirft.

The 16th, the Pilots of the *Joly*, *l' Aimable* and *la Belle*, went again to found, they found the Entrance eafy, and gave it under their Hands. The 17th, they fix'd Stakes to mark out the Way, that the Veffels might come fafe in. All Things feem'd to promife a happy Event.

The 18th, the Chevalier *d' Aire* came afhore, to confer with Monfieur *de la Sale*, who being defirous to have the Fly-boat *l' Aimable* come in that Day, order'd the moft weighty Things in her to be unloaded, as the Cannon, the Iron and fome other Things. It was my good Fortune that my Cheft ftood in the Way, and was alfo unloaded, but that Unlading could not be done till the next Day, being the 19th. That being perform'd, the Captain affirm'd it would go in at 8 Foot Water.

The 20th, Monfieur *de la Sale* fent Orders to that Captain to draw near the Bar, and to come in at high Water, of which a Signal fhould be given him ; he alfo order'd the Pilot of the Bark *la Belle* to go aboard the Flyboat, to be affifting when it came in. The Captain would not receive him aboard, faying, he could carry in his Ship without his Help. All thefe Precautions prov'd of no Ufe ; Monfieur *de la Sale* could not avert his ill Fate. He having taken Notice of a large Tree on the Bank of the River, which he judg'd fit to make a Canoe, fent 7 or 8 Workmen to hew it down, two of whom return'd fome Time after, in a great Fright, and told him, they had narrowly efcap'd being

D   taken

taken by a Company of Savages, and that they believ'd the others had fallen into their Hands. Monſieur *de la Sale* order'd us immediately to handle our Arms, and to march with Drums beating towards the Savages, who ſeeing us in that Poſture, fac'd about and went off.

Monſieur *de la Sale* being deſirous to join thoſe Savages, to endeavour to get ſome Information from them, order'd Ten of us to lay down our Arms and draw near them, making Signs to them, at the ſame Time, to come to us. When they ſaw us in that Poſture and unarm'd, moſt
Their Friendly Behaviour. of them alſo laid down their Bows and Arrows and came to meet us, carreſſing us after their Manner, and ſtroaking firſt their own Breaſts and then ours, then their own Arms and afterwards ours. By theſe Signs they gave us to underſtand that they had a Friendſhip for us, which they expreſs'd by laying their Hands on their Hearts, and we did the ſame on our Part.

Six or ſeven of thoſe Savages went along with us, and the reſt kept three of our Men, in the Nature of Hoſtages. Thoſe who went with us were made much of, but Monſieur *de la Sale* could learn nothing of them, either by Signs or otherwiſe ; all they could make us underſtand was, that there was good hunting of Bullocks in the Country. We obſerv'd, that their *Yea* conſiſted in a Cry, fetch'd from the Bottom of the Throat, not unlike the Call of a Hen to gather her Chickens. Monſieur *de la Sale* gave them ſome Knives, Hatchets and other Trifles, with which they ſeem'd well pleaſed, and went away.

Monſieur

Monſieur *de la Sale* was glad to be rid of
thoſe People, becauſe he was willing to be preſent when the Flyboat came in ; but his ill Fate
would not permit it. He thought fit to go himſelf along with thoſe Savages, and we follow'd
him, thinking to have found our Men in the
ſame Place where we left them; but perceiv'd on
the Contrary, that the Savages had carried
them away to their Camp, which was a League
and half from us, and Monſieur *de la Sablonniere*,
Lieutenant of Foot, being one of thoſe the Savages had taken with them. Monſieur *de la Sale*
reſolved to go himſelf to fetch him away, an
unhappy Thought which coſt him dear.

As we were on our Way towards the Camp
of the Savages, happenning to look towards the
Sea, we ſaw the Flyboat *l' Aimable* under Sail,
which the Savages who were with us admir'd,
and Monſieur *de la Sale* obſerving it narrowly,
told us, thoſe People ſteer'd wrong, and were
ſtanding towards the Shoals, which made him
very uneaſy, but ſtill we advanc'd. We arriv'd
at the Camp of the Savages, which ſtood upon *Their*
an Eminence, and conſiſted of about Fifty Cot- *Camp.*
tages made of ruſh Mats, and others of dry'd
Skins, and built with long Poles, bow'd round
at the Top, like great Ovens, and moſt of the
Savages ſitting about, as if they were upon the
Watch.

We were ſtill advancing into the Village,
when we heard a Cannon Shot, the Noiſe
whereof ſtruck ſuch a Dread among the Savages,
that they all fell flat upon the Ground ; but
Monſieur *de la Sale* and we were too ſenſible it
was a Signal that our Ship was aground, which
was confirm'd by ſeeing them furl their Sails ;

however

However we were gone too far to return; our Men muſt be had, and to that Purpoſe, we muſt proceed to the Hut of the Commander in Chief.

As ſoon as we arrived there, Monſr. *de la Sale* was introduc'd; many of the *Indian* Women came in, they were very deform'd and all naked, excepting a Skin girt about them, which hung down to their Knees. They would have led us to their Cottages, but Monſr. *de la Sale* had order'd us not to part, and to obſerve whether the *Indians* did not draw together, ſo that we kept together, ſtanding upon our Guard, and I was always with him.

Their Entertainment. They brought us ſome Pieces of Beef, both freſh and dry'd in the Air and Smoke, and Pieces of Porpois, which they cut with a Sort of Knife, made of Stone, ſetting one Foot upon it, and holding with one Hand, whilſt they cut with the other. We ſaw nothing of Iron among them. They had given our Men, that came with them, to eat, and Monſr. *de la Sale* being extraordinary uneaſy, we ſoon took Leave of them to return. At our going out, we obſerv'd about forty Canoes, ſome of them like thoſe Monſr. *de la Sale* had ſeen on the *Miſſiſipi*, which made him conclude he was not far from it.

L' Aimable caſt away. We ſoon arrived at our Camp, and found the Misfortune, Monſr. *de la Sale* had apprehended, was but too certain. The Ship was ſtranded on the Shoals. The ill Management of the Captain, or of the Pilot, who had not ſteer'd by the Stakes placed for that Purpoſe; the Cries of a Sailor poſted on the Main-top, who cry'd amain, *Loof*, which was to ſteer

towards

towards the Paſſage mark'd out, whilſt the
wicked Captain cry'd, *Come no nearer*, which was
to ſteer the contrary Courſe; the ſame Captain's
Carelefneſs in not dropping his Anchor, as ſoon
as the Ship touch'd, which would have prevented her ſticking aground; the Folly of low-
ering his Main-Sheet and hoiſting out his Sprit-
Sail, the better to fall into the Wind, and ſecure the Shipwreck; the Captain's refuſing to
admit the Pilot of the Bark *la Belle*, whom Monſieur *de la Sale* had ſent to aſſiſt him; the ſound-
ing upon the Shoals to no Purpoſe, and ſeveral other Circumſtances reported by the Ship's
Crew and thoſe who ſaw the Management,
were infallible Tokens and Proofs, that the
Miſchief had been done deſignedly and adviſe-
ably, which was one of the blackeſt and moſt
deteſtable Actions that Man could be guilty
of.

This Misfortune was ſo much the greater,
becauſe that Veſſel contain'd almoſt all the Ammunition, Utenſils, Tools and other Neceſſaries
for Monſr. *de la Sale*'s Enterprize and Settlement. He had need of all his Reſolution to
bear up againſt it; but his Intrepidity did not
forſake him, and he apply'd himſelf, without
grieving, to Remedy what might be. All the
Men were taken out of the Ship; he deſir'd
Monſieur *de Beaujeu* to lend him his long Boat,
to help ſave as much as might be. We began with Powder and Meal. About thirty Hog-
ſheads of Wine and Brandy were ſaved, and
Fortune being incens'd againſt us, two Things
contributed to the total Loſs of all the reſt:

The

The firſt was, that our Boat, which hung at
the Stern of the Ship run A-ground, was mali-
ciouſly ſtav'd in the Night, ſo that we had none
left but Monſieur *de Beaujeu*'s. The ſecond,
that the Wind blowing in from the Offing,
made the Waves run high, which beating violently againſt the Ship, ſplit her, and all the
light Goods were carry'd out at the opening,
by the Water. This laſt Misfortune happen'd
alſo in the Night. Thus every Thing fell out
moſt unhappily, for had that befallen in the
Day, Abundance of Things might have been
ſaved.

Whilſt we were upon this melancholly Employment, about an hundred, or an hundred and
twenty of the Natives came to our Camp, with
their Bows and Arrows. Monſieur *de la Sale*
order'd us to handle our Arms, and ſtand upon
our Guard. About twenty of thoſe *Indians*
mix'd themſelves among us, to obſerve what we
had ſaved of the Shipwreck, upon which, there
were ſeveral Sentinels, to let none come near
the Powder.

The reſt of the *Indians* ſtood in Parcels, or
Pelotons. Monſr. *de la Sale*, who was acquainted with their Ways, order'd us to obſerve their
Behaviour, and to take Nothing from them,
which neverthelefs did not hinder ſome of our
Men from receiving ſome Pieces of Meat. Some
Time after, when the *Indians* were about departing, they made Signs to us to go a Hunting with them; but beſides that, there was ſufficient Cauſe to ſuſpect them, we had enough other
Buſineſs to do. However we ask'd, whether they
would barter for any of their Canoes; which
they agreed to. The Sieur *Barbier* went along
                                                    with

with them, purchas'd two for Hatchets and brought them.

Some Days after, we perceiv'd a Fire in the Country, which spread it self and burnt the dry Weeds, still drawing towards us; whereupon, Monsr. *de la Sale* made all the Weeds and Herbs that were about us, be pull'd up, and particularly all about the Place where the Powder was. Being desirous to know the Occasion of that Fire, he took about twenty of us along with him, and we march'd that Way, and even beyond the Fire, without seeing any Body. We perceiv'd that it run towards the *W. S. W.* and judg'd it had begun about our first Camp, and at the Village next the Fire.

Having spy'd a Cottage near the Bank of a Lake, we drew towards it, and found an old Woman in it, who fled as soon as she saw us; but having overtaken and given her to understand, that we would do her no Harm, she return'd to her Cottage, where we found some Pitchers of Water, of which we all drank. Some Time after we saw a Canoe coming, in which were two Women and a Boy, who being landed, and perceiving we had done the old Woman no *Odd Salutation.* Harm, came and imbraced us in a very particular Manner, blowing upon our Ears and making Signs to give us to understand, that their People were a hunting.

A few Minutes after, seven or eight of the *Indians* appeared, who, it is likely, had hid themselves among the Weeds when they saw us coming. Being come up they saluted us, after the same Manner, as the Women had done, which made us laugh. We staid there some Time with them. Some of our Men barter'd

Knives

Knives for Goats Skins, after which we return'd
to our Camp ; Being come thither, Monfieur
de la Sale made me go aboard the Bark *la Belle*,
vvhere he had imbark'd Part of the Povvder,
vvith pofitive Orders not to carry, or permit
any Fire to be made there, having fufficient
Caufe to fear every thing, after vvhat had hapned. For this Reafon they carry'd me and
all that vvere vvith me, our Meat every Day.

During this time it was that *l'Aimable* opening in the Night, the next Morning we faw
all the light Things that were come out of it
floating about, and Monfieur *de la Sale* fent Men
every Way, who gather'd up about 30 Casks
of Wine and Brandy, and fome of Flefh, Meal
and Grain.

When we had gather'd all, as well what had
been taken out of the Ship-wreck'd Veffel as
what could be pick'd up in the Sea, the next
Thing was to regulate the Provifions we had
left proportionably to the Number of Men we
were ; and there being no more Bisket, Meal
was deliver'd out, and with it we made Hafty
Pudding with Water, which was none of the
beft ; fome large Beans and *India* Corn, part of
which had taken wet ; and every thing was di-
ftributed very difcreetly. We were much in-
commoded for want of Kettles, but Monfieur
de Beaujeu gave Monfieur *de la Sale* one, and he
order'd another to be brought from the Bark
la Belle, by which means we were well ferv'd.

We were ftill in want of Canoes. Monfieur
de la Sale fent to the Camp of the *Indians* to
barter for fome, and they who went thither
obferv'd, that thofe People had made their Advantage of our Ship-wreck, and had fome Bales
of

of *Normandy* Blankets, and they faw feveral
Women had cut them in two and made Petti-
coats of them.   They alfo faw Bits of Iron of
the Ship that was caft away, and return'd
immediately to make their Report to Monfieur
de la Sale, who faid we muft endeavour to get
fome Canoes in Exchange, and refolv'd to fend
thither again the next Day. Monfieur *du Hamel*,
Enfign to Monfr. *de Beaujeu*, offer'd to go up in
his Boat, which Monfieur *de la Sale* agreed to,
and order'd Meffieurs *Moranget*, his Nephew,
Defloges, *Oris*, *Gayen*, and fome others to bear
him Company.

No fooner were thofe Gentlemen, who were
more Hot than Wife, landed, but they went up
to the Camp of the *Indians*, with their Arms
in their Hands, as if they had intended to force
them, whereupon feveral of thofe People fled.
Going into the Cottages, they found others, to
whom Monfieur *du Hamel* endeavour'd to fignify by Signs, that he would have the Blankets
they had found reftor'd ; but the Misfortune
was, that none of them underftood one another.
The *Indians* thought it their beft Way to withdraw, leaving behind them fome Blankets and
Skins of Beafts, which thofe Gentlemen took
away, and finding fome Canoes in their Return
they feiz'd two, and got in, to bring them
away.

But having no Oars, none of them knowing
how to manage thofe Canoes, and having only
fome pitiful Poles, which they could not tell
the right Ufe of, and the Wind being alfo a-
gainft them, they made little Way ; which the
Sieur *du Hamel*, who was in his Boat perceiving,
and that Night drew on, he made the beft of
his

his Way, forfook them and return'd to the Camp.

Thus Night came upon them, which oblig'd thofe unexperienc'd Canoe Men, being thoroughly tir'd, to go afhore to take fome Reft, and the Weather being cold, they lighted a Fire, about which they laid them down and *The* Indians *take* fell afleep ; the Sentinel they had appointed *Revenge.* doing the fame. The *Indians* returning to their Camp, and perceiving our Men had carry'd away two Canoes, fome Skins and Blankets, took it for a Declaration of a War, refolv'd to be reveng'd, and difcovering an unufual Fire, prefently concluded that our Men had halted there. A confiderable Number of them repair'd to the Place, without making the leaft Noife, found our carelefs People faft afleep, wrap'd up in their Blankets, and fhot a full Volley of their Arrows upon them all together on a Sudden, having firft given their ufual Shout before they fall on.

Sieurs Oris and *Defloges* kill'd. The Sieur *Moranget* awaking with the Noife, and finding himfelf wounded, ftarted up and fir'd his Piece fuccefsfully enough, fome others did the like, whereupon the Natives fled. The Sieur *Moranget* came to give us the Alarm, though he was fhot through one of his Arms, below the Shoulder, and had another flanting Wound on the Breaft. Monfieur *de la Sale* immediately fent fome arm'd Men to the Place, who could not find the *Indians*, but when Day appear'd, they found the Sieurs *Oris* and *Defloges* dead upon the Spot, the Sieur *Gayen* much hurt, and the reft all fafe and found.

This

This Difafter, which happen'd the Night of the 5th of *March*, very much afflicted Monfieur *de la Sale*; but he chiefly lamented Monfieur *Defloges* a fprightly Youth, who ferv'd well; but in fhort, it was their own Fault, and contrary to the Charge given them, which was to be watchful and upon their Guard. We were under Apprehenfions for Meffieurs *Moranget* and *Gayen*, left the Arrows fhould be poifon'd. It afterwards appear'd they were not, however Monfieur *Moranget*'s Cure prov'd difficult, becaufe fome fmall Veffel was cut.

The Confequences of this Misfortune, together with the Concern, moft of the beft Perfons who had follow'd Monfieur *de la Sale* were under, fupported the Defign of thofe who were for returning to *France* and forfaking him, of which Number were Monfieur *Dairmaville*, a Prieft of the Seminary of St. *Sulpice*, the Sieur *Minet*, Engineer and fome others. The common Difcourfes of Monfieur *de la Sale*'s Enemies tending to difcredit his Conduct, and to reprefent the pretended Rafhnefs of his Enterprize, contributed confiderably tovvards the Defertion; but his Refolution prevailing, he heard and waited all Events vvith Patience, and alvvays gave his Orders, vvithout appearing the leaft difcompos'd.

He caus'd the Dead to be brought to our Camp, and bury'd them Honourably, the Cannon fupplying the Want of Bells, and then confider'd of making fome fafer Settlement. He caus'd all that had been fav'd from the Shipvvreck, to be brought together into one Place, threvv up Intrenchments about it, to fecure his Effects, and perceiving that the

Water

Water of the River, where we were, roul'd down violently into the Sea, he fancy'd that might be one of the Branches of the *Miſſiſipi*, and propos'd to go up it, to ſee whether he could find any Tokens of it, or of the Marks he had left, when he went down by Land to the Mouth of it.

Debates between the Commanders.

In the mean Time, Monſieur *de Beaujeu* was preparing to depart: The Chevalier *de Aire* had many Conferences with Monſieur *de la Sale* about ſeveral things, the latter demanded of Monſieur *de Beaujeu*, particularly the Cannon and Ball which were aboard the *Joly*, and had been deſign'd for him; which Monſieur *de Beaujeu* refus'd, alledging that all thoſe things lay at the Bottom of the Hold, and that he could not rummage it without evident Danger of periſhing; tho', at the ſame time, he knew we had Eight Pieces of Cannon and not one Bullet.

Mr. de la Sale much wrong'd.

I know not how that Affair was decided between them; but am ſure he ſuffer'd the Captain of the Fly-boat *l'Aimable* to imbark aboard Monſieur *de Beaujeu*, tho' he deſerv'd to be moſt ſeverely puniſh'd, had Juſtice been done him. His Crew follow'd him, contrary to what Monſieur *de Beaujeu* had promis'd, that he would not receive a Man of them. All that Monſieur *de la Sale* could do, tho' ſo much wrong'd, was to write to *France*, to Monſieur *de Saignelay*, Miniſter of State, whom he acquainted with all the Particulars, as I was inform'd, when I return'd, and he gave the Packet to Monſieur *de Beaujeu*, who ſail'd away for *France*.

Mr. de Beaujeu leaves him

Having loſt the Notes I took at that time, and being forc'd to rely much upon Memory for what I now write, I ſhall not pretend to be

any

any longer exact in the Dates, for fear of
mistaking, and therefore I cannot be positive
as to the Day of Monsieur *de Beaujeu*'s Departure, but believe it was the 14th of *March*,
1685.

When Monsr. *de Beaujeu* vvas gone, we fell
to Work to make a Fort, of the Wreck of the
Ship that had been cast away, and many Pieces
of Timber the Sea threw up; and during that
Time, several Men deserted, which added to
Monsieur *de la Sale*'s Affliction. A *Spaniard* and
a *French* Man stole away and fled, and were never more heard of. Four or five others follow'd
their Example, but Monsieur *de la Sale* having
timely Notice, sent after them, and they were
brought back. One of them was condemn'd to
Death, and the others to serve the King ten
Years in that Country.

When our Fort was well advanc'd, Monsr.
de la Sale resolv'd to clear his Doubts, and to go
up the River, where we were, to know whether it was not an Arm of the *Mississipi*, and accordingly order'd fifty Men to attend him, of
which Number were Monsr. *Cavelier*, his Brother, and Monsr. *Chedeville*, both Priests, two
Recolet Fryars, and several Voluntiers, who
set out in five Canoes we had, with the necef-
sary Provisions. There remain'd in the Fort a-
bout an hundred and thirty Persons, and Monsr
de la Sale gave me the Command of it, with Orders not to have any Commerce with the Natives, but to fire at them if they appear'd.

Whilst Monsr. *de la Sale* was absent, I caus'd
an Oven to be built, vvhich vvas a great Help
to us, and employ'd my self in finishing the
Fort, and putting it in a Posture to vvith-
stand

*Mar.*168 $

stand the *Indians*, who came frequently in the Night to range about us, howling like Wolves and Dogs ; but two or three Mufquet Shots put them to Flight. It happen'd one Night, that having fir'd fix or feven Shot, Monfieur *de la Sale*, vvho vvas not far from us, heard *Returns* them, and being in Pain about it, he return'd with fix or feven Men, and found all Things in a good Pofture.

He told us he had found a good Country, fit to fow and plant all Sorts of Grain, abounding in Beeves and wild Fowl ; that he *Sets out a-* defign'd to erect a Fort farther up the River, *gain.* and accordingly he left me Orders to fquare out as much Timber as I could get, the Sea cafting up much upon the Shore. He had given the fame Orders to the Men he had left on the Spot, feven or eight of whom, detach'd from the reft, being bufy at that Work, and feeing a Number of the Natives, fled, and unadvifeably left their Tools behind them. Monfieur *de la Sale* returning thither, found a Paper made faft to a Reed, vvhich gave him Notice of that Accident, vvhich he was concern'd at, becaufe of the Tools, not fo much for the Value of the Lofs, as becaufe it was furnifhing the Natives with fuch Things as they might afterwards make Ufe of againft us.

About the Beginning of *April*, we were a- *A Spanifh* larm'd by a Veffel which appear'd at Sea, near *Veffel ap-* enough to difcern the Sails, and we fuppofed *pears.* they might be *Spaniards*, who had heard of our Coming and were ranging the Coaft to find us out. That made us ftand upon our Guard, to keep within the Fort, and fee that our Arms
were

were fit for Service. We afterwards saw two
Men in that Vessel, who instead of coming to
uss, went towards the other Point, and by
that Means pass'd on, without perceiving us.

Having one Day observ'd, that the Water
work'd and bubbled up, and afterwards per-
ceiving it was occasion'd by the Fish skipping   *Plenty of*
from Place to Place, I caused a Net to be   *Fish taken.*
brought, and we took a prodigious Quantity of
Fish, among which were many *Dorado*'s, or
Gilt-Heads, Mullets and others about as big
as a Herring, which afforded us good Food for
several Days. This Fishery, which I caused to
be often follow'd, was a great Help towards
our Subsistance.

About that Time, and on *Easter-day* that
Year, an unfortunate Accident befel Monsieur
le Gros. After Divine Service he took a Gun
to go kill Snipes about the Fort. He shot   *Rattle*
one, which fell into a Marsh, he took off his *Snake*
Shoes and Stockings to fetch it out, and re-   *bites Mr.*
turning, through Carelesness trod upon a Rat- *le Gros,*
tle Snake, so call'd, because it has a Sort of
Scale on the Tail, which makes a Noise. The
Serpent bit him a little above the Ankle, he
was carefully dress'd and look'd after, yet
after having endur'd very much, he dy'd at
last, as I shall mention in its Place. Another
more unlucky Accident befell us, one of our
Fishermen swimming about the Net to gather
the Fish, was carry'd away by the Current,
and could not be help'd by us.

Our Men sometimes went about several   *May* 1685
little Salt Water Lakes, that were near our
Fort, and found on the Banks a Sort of flat
Fishes, like Turbots asleep, which they struck
with

with sharp pointed Sticks, and they were good Food. Providence also shew'd us that there was Salt made by the Sun, upon several little Salt Water Pools there were in divers Places, for having observ'd that there grew on them a Sort of white Substance, like the Cream upon Milk, I took Care every Day to send and fetch that Scum off, which prov'd to be a very white and good Salt, whereof I gather'd a Quantity, and it did us good Service.

Some of our Hunters having seen a Parcel of wild Goats running as if they vvere frighted, judg'd they were pursued by the *Indians*, and came for Refuge to the Fort, and to give me Notice. Accordingly some Time after, we discover'd a Parcel of Natives, who came and po-

sted themselves on an Eminence, within Cannon Shot, some of them drew off from the rest and approach'd the Fort by the Way of the Downs. I caused our Men immediately to handle their Arms, and wet Blankets to be laid on our Huts, to prevent their being burnt by the Fire the Savages sometimes shoot with their Arrows. All this Time those who had separated themselves from the rest, being three in Number, still drew nearer, making Signs for us to go to them; but Monsieur *de la Sale* had forbid me having any Commerce with them; however, since they had neither Bows nor Arrows, we made Signs to them to draw near, which they did without hesitating.

We went out to meet them, Monsieur *Moranget* made them sit down, and they gave us to understand by Signs, that their People were hunting near us; being able to make no more of what they said, Monsieur *Moranget* was for

knocking

knocking out their Brains, to revenge their *June* 1685
having murder'd our Companions, but I would
not confent to it, fince they had come confiding
in us. I made Signs to them to be gone, which
they did as faft as they could, fome fmall Shot
we fir'd into the Air making them run, and a
Cannon Shot, I pointed towards the rifing
Ground, where the reft were, put them all to
Flight.

These Accidents made us double our Guards,
fince we were at open War with that crafty
Nation, which let flip no Opportunity to fur-
prize us, and therefore Penalties were appointed for fuch as fhould be found afleep upon Sentinel; the Wooden-Horfe was fet up for them
without Remiffion; and by Means of fuch Precautions we fav'd our Lives.

Thus we fpent the reft of the Month, till
the Beginning of *June*. In the mean Time,
Monfieur *de la Sale* had begun to make another
Settlement, in the Place he before told us of,
looking upon it as better, becaufe it was further up the Country. To that Purpofe he fent
to us the Sieur *de Villeperdry* with two Canoes *Second*
and Orders for the Sieur *Moranget* to repair to *Settlement*
him, if he were recover'd, and that all the Men
fhould march, except 30 of the ableft to make
a good Defence, who were to ftay with me in
the Fort. The reft being feventy Perfons, as
well Men and Women as Children, fet out
with the Sieur *Moranget*; and we being but a
fmall Number remaining, I caufed the Fort to
be brought into a lefs Compafs, to fave pofting
fo many Sentinels.

Our little Company began to take Satisfaction in the Eafe of getting and the Nature of our
E   Provifions

Proviſions, which a greater Number has more
Difficulty to be ſupply'd with, and which we
had Plenty of, by Means of Hunting and Fiſhing,
thoſe being our principal Employments, and
we liv'd well enough contented, expecting to be
remov'd.   However there were ſome Malecon-
tents, who reſolv'd to deſert; but finding a
Difficuly to put it in Execution, for that they
could neither get Arms, nor Powder nor Ball,
becauſe the Sieur *le Gros* and I kept all lock'd
up, and were very vigilant, that none might be
laviſhly ſpent, they took the cruel Reſolution
to rid themſelves of us.

That bloody Maſſacre was to begin by me,
when I was aſleep, and then to proceed to the
Sieur *le Gros*, who lay in the Magazine, or
Warehouſe, and was in no Condition to defend
himſelf, becauſe his Leg was ſtill ſwolen, and
put him to much Pain.   The Execution was to
be by ſtabbing.   One of the Conſpirarors re-
veal'd this to the Sieur *Davault*, a Hunter, who
immediately came and accquainted me.   I did
not juſt then take Notice of what I had been
told; but in the Evening, when they return'd
from hunting, I cauſed one to be ſecur'd, who
preſently confeſs'd all.   His Accomplice was
alſo ſeiz'd, and it was very troubleſom to ſecure them till the Time when we ſhould remove.

About the Middle of *July*, the Bark *la Belle*
came and anchor'd near us.   An Order was
brought me from Monſieur *de la Sale*, directing
me to put aboard it all the Effects that were in
our Fort, to make a Float of the Timber I had
cauſed to be ſquar'd, if Time would permit, if
not to bury it in the Ground.   Every Man ſet
his

his Hand to the Work, with all possible Dili- *July* 1685
gence, and our two Prisoners were put aboard,
as was also Monsieur *le Gros* and his Surgeon,
with all our Effects.

The Float was begun with immense Labour;
but the Weather proving very Stormy, and
holding very long, I was oblig'd to cause what
had been done to be taken in Pieces, and to
bury the Timber in the Sand, the best we could,
that the Natives might not find it.

We then set out towards the Place where *The first*
the *Indians* had been encamp'd, when Monsieur *Fort aban-*
de la Sale went the first time to see them. We *don'd.*
found no Creature, and lay there that Night.
and so proceeded along the Sea Coast, without
any Accident, to the Camp of the Sieur *Hurie*,
which was a Post in the Way, where Monsieur
de la Sale had order'd all our Effects to be laid
up. It had no other Inclosure but Chests and
Barrels; but there was nothing to fear from
the *Europeans*.

We spent the Night at that Post, and two *Ill Posture*
Canoes coming thither the next Morning, I *of the 2d.*
went aboard one of them, with Part of my *Settlement*
Company, and join'd Monsieur *de la Sale* the
next Day, at the Place where he had resolv'd
to make his new Settlement. I gave him an
Account of all that had happen'd, and was
amaz'd to see Things so ill begun and so little
advanc'd. As for the Plantation, the Seed
and Grain put into the Ground, was either lost
through Drought, or eaten by Birds or Beasts.
There were several Dead, and among them the
Sieur *de Villeperdry*; many sick, and of that
Number Monsieur *Cavalier* the Priest; no Shelter but a little square Place stak'd in, where the
E 2   Powder

July 1685 Powder was and some Casks of Brandy, many other Inconveniences there were, which made all Things appear in a miserable Condition.

It was requisite to think of building a large Lodgment, Monsieur *de la Sale* design'd it, but the Difficulty was to get proper Timber for Building. There was a little Wood, where a good Quantity might be had, but it was a League up the Country, and we had neither Carts nor Horses to carry it; however Monsr. *de la Sale* sent Workmen thither, with others to guard them. The Trees were cut down and squar'd, but the Carpenters were so ignorant, that Monsr. *de la Sale* was forc'd to act the Master Builder, and to mark out the Pieces for the Work he design'd. Some of those Pieces of Timber were dragg'd to the Camp, over the Grass and Weeds the Plain was cover'd with; afterwards the Carriage of a Gun was made use of; but all cost so much Labour, that the ablest Men were quite spent.

Hard La-bour.

This excessive Toil, the poor Sustenance the labouring Men had, and that often retrench'd as a Penalty for having fail'd in doing their Duty; the Uneasiness Monsieur *de la Sale* was under to see nothing succeed as he had imagin'd, and which often made him insult the Men, when there was little Reason for it; All these things together afflicted very many so sensibly, that they visibly declin'd, and above thirty dy'd. The Loss of so many Men was follow'd by that of the Master Carpenter, who was returning one Evening with me; but I happening to step aside to kill some wild Fowl, when I came to our Habitation I found him not, and it was never known what became of him; an

Carpenter lost.

Accident

Accident which added to our Vexation, for tho' *Aug. 1685* he had but little Skill at his Trade, yet we stood in Need of him.

Notwithstanding all those Disappointments, enough Timber was carry'd or rather dragg'd, to build the House Monsieur *de la Sale* design'd, and he was himself the Architect. He mark'd out the Lengths, the Tenants and Mortises, and made good the Defect of th e Workmen and calling to Mind that I had bury'd several Pieces of Timber at our first Habitation, which might be of Use, he order'd me to take two Canoes and 20 Men, to go fetch them, in the Bark *la Belle*, which was with us.

Being come to the Place, we found the Natives had discover'd our Timber, and carry'd away some Planks, to pick out the Nails there were in them, which they value very much, to point their Arrows. We labour'd to make a Float, loaded the Bark *la Belle* with the rest of the Planks and other Effects, and set out again. Some of the Natives appear'd whilst we were at Work, but seeing us advance towards them, with our Arms in our Hands, they fled.

We return'd safe to Monsieur *de la Sale*, who *Second Set-* was glad to see us, tho' we had lost one of the *tlement.* Canoes, for want of its being well made fast to the Float; but the Timber we brought was a mighty Help towards carrying on his Design, and much fitter than that we had hew'd in the Wood, with so much Labour; so that this Timber occasion'd the raising another Structure contiguous to the former. All was cover'd with Planks, and Bullocks Hides over them. The Apartments were divided, and all of them well cover'd.

cover'd. The Stores had a Place apart, and that Dwelling had the Name of St. *Lewis* given it, as well as the Neighbouring Bay.

The Sieur *le Gros*, who had remain'd aboard the Bark *le Belle*, ever fince the firft Voyage fhe made to our former Habitation, was carry'd *Mr.* le afhore to the new One, and his Leg ftill fwell-*Gros dies* ing, the Surgeon was apprehenfive of a Morti-*and others* fication, and advis'd him to confent to have it cut off. He did fo, tho' with Regret, the Operation was made, but a Fever follow'd immediately, and he liv'd but two Days, dying on the Feaft of the Decollation of St. *John Baptift*, much lamented by all Men, and particularly by Monfieur *de la Sale*, to whom he was very ferviceable, by reafon of his general Knowledge, and his particular Fidelity towards him. Monfieur *Carpentier*, Son to the Mafter of the Works and the Sieur *Thibault*, both of *Roan*, and fome others, dy'd about the fame time.

Monfieur *de la Sale* being defirous to take a Progrefs, to find his fatal *Miffifipi* River, and only expecting the Recovery of his Brother Monfieur *Cavalier*, who was to bear him Company, he began to make fome Preparations towards it, and in the mean time, took fome fmall Journeys of four or five Leagues about, but could learn nothing further, than that it was a very fine Country, hem'd in on one Side by a fmall Mountain, which appear'd at about Fifteen or Twenty Leagues diftance; beautify'd with very fine Trees, and water'd by many little Rivers, whereof that, on which we had Built our Habitation was the leaft. *River of* We call'd it *la Riviere aux Bœufs*, that is the *Bullocks.* River of Bullocks, by reafon of the great Number

ber

ber of them there was about it. These Bullocks are very like ours, there are Thousands of them, but instead of Hair they have a very long curl'd Sort of Wool.

Monsieur *de la Sale* Studying all Ways to find out the River *Mississipi*, imagin'd it might fall into the adjacent Bay, and resolv'd to go view all the Coasts about it, and to make use of the Bark *la Belle*. Accordingly he order'd me to repair to the said Bark, with five Men and a Canoe, into which he put his Cloaths, and other Effects in several Chests.

That short Voyage was very troublesome to us, by reason of the foul Weather, with contrary Winds and Storms, which had like to have overwhelm'd us, and what was still worse, we did not find the Bark, where we had left her. We went on a League further, to no Purpose, and Provisions beginning to fall short, because we had been six Days on the Way, instead of three, we resolv'd to return to the Place from whence we came.

Monsieur *de la Sale* seeing us return at a distance, came to meet us. Our Report troubled him for the Bark, which he stood in need of, so that he resolv'd to go himself to seek her, imbark'd in a Canoe, and sent me another Way, in another. After having wander'd about all that Day, the next Night and the Day following, we at last perceiv'd her, where she lay under Shelter in a little Creek, having been in Danger of Perishing by the foul Weather we had been in, and had lost her Boat, which was not well made fast.

Boat of the Bark lost.

The

The Bark was also discover'd by Monsieur *de la Sale*, who was on the other side, which made him draw near and land, whence he sent his Canoe to the said Bark, and Monsieur *Moranget* who commanded it, went aboard to meet him. The Loss of the Boat troubled Monsieur *de la Sale*, I sent a Canoe to bring him, but to no Purpose; however the Trunks were put aboard the Bark.

What Stores they had.

Monsieur *Cavalier* the Priest, being recover'd, Monsieur *de la Sale* prepar'd to set out with all Speed. He was pleas'd to Honour me with the Command, during his Absence, and left me an Inventory of all that was in our Habitation, consisting of Eight Pieces of Cannon, two Hundred Firelocks, as many Cutlaces, an Hundred Barrels of Powder, three Thousand Weight of Ball, about three Hundred Weight of other Lead, some Bars of Iron, twenty Packs of Iron to make Nails, some Iron Work and Tools, as Hatchets and the like.

As for Provisions, all that were left me amounted to twenty Casks of Meal, one Cask and a half of Wine, three Quarters of a Cask of Brandy, and for living Creatures some few Swine, a Cock and a Hen; which is very short of what has been Publish'd by the Author of a Book entituled, *The first Establishment in New France*: but the Reason of it is, that he compiled his Work upon the Credit of Relations, which were as false as to the Point of the Ammunition and Provisions, remaining in our Habitation, when Monsieur *de la Sale* set out that Time, as concerning the Fort well condition'd, and the Magazines or Storehouses under Ground, which are all imaginary, there being Nothing but the

House

House I have mention'd, pallisado'd, with some old Stakes.

Monsr. *de la Sale* farther order'd me not to receive any Man of those he took along with him, unless they brought an Order from him in Writing; nor to hold or admit of any Communication with the Natives, but rather to fire upon them, and some other Particulars he thought fit to be obferv'd. He had made himself a Coat of Mail with small Laths, to secure himself against the Arrows, which he took along with him, he also took the Canoes, and promis'd to send me one back. Five Cannon Shot were the Signal of his Departure.

He took his Way along the lower Part of the River, to march by Land along the neighbouring Bay, which was call'd of St. *Lewis*, the Canoes keeping within Sight. I was left in the Habitation with thirty four Persons, Men, Women and Children, and of that Number were three *Recolet* Friars, the Sieur *Hurie*, who was to command in my Absence, one of the Sieurs *Duhaut*, the Sieurs *Thibault* and a Surgeon. *Monsr. de la Sale goes out to discover. St. Lewis's Bay.*

Our Provisions being very small, and it being requisite to spare them, for the Sick, we were oblig'd to apply our selves to Fishing and Shooting. Both of them at first prov'd very unsuccessful, especially the latter; because we were not yet well vers'd in them, and Monsieur *de la Sale* had taken our Huntsman along with him ; but at length, Necessity made us more expert. We kill'd Beeves, some of which I caus'd to be dry'd, and they were a considerable Help to subsist us.

Some

Some Days after, the Canoe Monfieur *de la Sale* had promis'd me, arrived with three Soldiers, who brought us the News of the Lofs of the Huntfman Monfieur *de la Sale* had taken along with him, and who had been found dead with Cold in a Ditch, where he had lain down to reft after hunting, which troubled us all very much. They .alfo inform'd us, that Monfr. *de la Sale* advancing towards fome Dwellings the Natives had abandon'd, after a fmall Refiftance, fome of whom had been wounded as they fled, they had taken and brought a Girl and a Woman, who was fhot thro' the Thigh, of which fhe dy'd:

*Dec.*1685 The Canoe was a great Help to us to carry what we kill'd, which being brought to our Habitation, found Employment, for all Perfons, fome to flea, others to cut up, and others to dry it. At other Times, I fet fome of our Men to throw up a Trench about our Habitation.

Thus we fpent our Time, till about the *Jan.*1686 Middle of *January,* 1686, when being all, one Evening, in our Manfion, the Sentinel came in to acquaint me, that he heard a Voice towards the River ; fome Men ran thither immediately, and found a Man in a Canoe, crying, *Dominick,* which was the Name of young *Duhaut,* who was with us. The Sight of that made me apprehenfive left fome Difafter was befallen Monfr. *de la Sale.* I drew near, and perceiv'd it was *Duhaut* the Elder, that was return'd.

I ask'd, him whether he had any Letters from Monfieur *de la Sale,* he anfwer'd, he had not. It gave me fome Uneafinefs, confidering I was forbid admitting any Man without an
Or-

Order in Writing, and I was almoſt reſolv'd to
ſecure him ; but the Account he gave me of the
Occaſion of his returning wholly clear'd him.
I admitted him, and he told me the whole
Matter as follows.

Monſr. *de la Sale*, having ſtaid ſome Time on
the Sea Shore, near the Place where the Bark
was at Anchor he reſolv'd to try the Anchor-
ing Places of the Coaſts round about, to know
how near the Bark *le Belle* might come. To that
Purpoſe he ſent the Pilot with 5 of the beſt Men
to ſound.

The Pilot did as he was order'd, he ſounded
and obſerved the proper Places to come near ſeveral Coaſts. At Night he and his Men being in all likelyhood tir'd, they thought fit to go
Aſhore and lie upon the Land. They made a
Fire, perhaps to dreſs ſome Meat ; but neglecting to ſtand upon their Guard, they were
ſurpriz'd, and all ſix of them kill'd by the Savages ; who alſo broke their Canoe, and thus
reveng'd themſelves for the Irruption Monſr. *de
la Sale* had lately made among them.

More Time being elaps'd than Monſieur *de
la Sale* had allotted thoſe Men to return, he
grew uneaſy, and went himſelf along the Coaſt,
to ſee if any News could be had of them, and
keeping along the Shore, he found the ſad Remains of thoſe unfortunate Wretches, whoſe
Carcaſſes ſcatter'd about, were torn and almoſt
devour'd by Wolves or wild Dogs, a Spectacle
which went to his Heart.

However this Loſs, which afflicted him, and
particularly for the Sake of the Pilot, who was
an able Man, did not quite caſt him down ; but
exerting himſelf againſt his Misfortunes, he
caus'd

*Jan.*1686 caus'd Fleſh to be dry'd, and with that and the other Proviſions he victuall'd the Bark *la Belle.* He caus'd it to advance into the Bay, put a good Number of Men on Board to ſecure it, among whom were Monſieur *Chedeville*, the Prieſt, and *Planteroſe* of *Roan*, and order'd them to ſtir from that Place till they heard from him, and not to go Aſhore, unleſs with a good Guard and neceſſary Precautions.

Next, he choſe out Twenty Men, imbark'd on two Canoes he had left, and being come Aſhore, caus'd the Canoes to be ſunk in the River, and every Man to take up his Bundle, conſiſting of Arms, Tools, ſome Utenſils for the Kitchin, a few Goods, to trade with the Natives, if he ſhould find any ſociable, and ſo advanc'd into the Country, to try if any Notice could be had of the *Miſſiſipi.*

After ſeveral Days March, they came to a good pleaſant River, which they afterwards call'd *la Maligne.* Monſieur *de la Sale* marching at the Head of the Company, and having order'd Monſieur *Moranget* to keep in the Rear; it happen'd that *Duhaut* ſtopping to mend his Snapſack and his Shoes, which were in a bad Condition; the Sieur *Moranget* coming up, commanded him to march, he deſired him to ſtay a little. *Moranget* would not, but held on his Way; *Duhaut* follow'd ſome Time after, but having ſtay'd too long, he could not overtake the Company, and found himſelf about Night fall in a Plain full of Weeds, where there were ſeveral Tracks of the Way Cattle had gone, but knew not which of them to take. He fir'd his Piece ſeveral Times, without hearing

La Ma-
ligne *Ri-*
ver.

ing any thing of his Company, and was oblig'd to pass the Night in that same Place.

In the Morning he shot again, spent the Day and Night again in that Place, so that not knowing what to do, he return'd the same Way he had gone, and after a Month's March, for he travell'd only by Night, for Fear of meeting with the Savages, living upon what he kill'd with much Difficulty and Danger, having before spent all his own Provisions; at length after most unaccountable Hardships and Sufferings, he arriv'd at the Place where the Canoes had been funk. He took one of them up, with incredible Labour, and too long to relate, and so came to our Habitation of St. *Lewis*. Thus it pleas'd God that he who was to be one of the Murderers of Monsieur *de la Sale*, should come off safe, and surmount almost infinite Dangers.

Strange Adventure

This Account, which seem'd to carry the Face of Probability, prevail'd with me to receive the Sieur *Duhaut*, and in Reality I could do no otherwise, and I made it my Business to examine into his Behaviour, but could find Nothing to lay to his Charge. We continued some Time longer as we had been before; during the which, I caus'd another little Wooden Structure to be made, of Timber, I had got together, and in it I lodg'd the Women and Maidens by themselves. Having hitherto said Nothing of the Situation of our Dwelling of St. *Lewis*, nor of the Nature of the Country we were in, I will here venture upon a plain but true Description.

We were in about the 27th Degree of North Latitude, two Leagues up the Country, near

the

Description of the Country and Dwelling at St. Lewis.
The Land.

the Bay of St. *Lewis* and the Bank of the River *aux Bœufs*, on a little Hillock, whence we discover'd vast and beautiful Plains, extending very far to the Westward, all level and full of Greens, which afford Pasture to an infinite Number of Beeves and other Creatures.

Turning from the West to the Southward, there appear'd other Plains adorn'd with several little Woods of severalSorts of Trees. Towards the South and East was the Bay, and the Plains that hem it in from the East; to the Northward, was the River running along by a little Hill, beyond which there were other large Plains, with some little Tufts of Wood at small Distances, terminating in a Border of Wood, which seem'd to us to be very high.

Living Creatures.

Between that little Hill and our Dwelling, was a Sort of Marsh, and in it Abundance of wild Foul, as Curlies, Water-Hens and other Sorts. In the Marsh there were little Pools full of Fish. We had also an infinite Number of Beeves, wild Goats, Rabbits, Turkeys, Bustards, Geese, Swans, Feldifares, Plovers, Teal, Partridges and many other Sorts of Fowl fit to eat, and among them one call'd *le grand Gosier*, or, the great Gullet, because it has a very large one; another as big and Fleshy as a Pullet, which we called the *Spatula*, because it's Beak is shap'd like one, and the Feathers of it being of a pale Red, are very beautiful.

Fish.

As for Fish, we had several Sorts in the River and in the Lakes I have mention'd. The River afforded a Sort of Barbles, differing from ours in Roundness, in their having three Bones sticking out, one on the Back, the others on each Side of the Head, and in the Flesh, which

is

The 18th, we were surpriz'd to see several
Women come into our Cottage, their Faces
all besmear'd with Earth, and they set up their
Throats, singing several Songs as loud as they
were able, whereof we understood not one
Word. That done, they fell a Dancing in a
Ring, and we could not tell, what to think of
that Rejoicing, which lasted full three Hours;
after which we were inform'd, they had receiv'd Advice of the Victory obtain'd by their
Warriors over their Enemies. The Dance
concluded, those in the Cottage gave some
Bits of Tabacco to those without.

May 1687

Women re-
joice at
Victory.

The same Day, about Noon, we saw him
that had brought the News, who affirm'd they
had kill'd at least Forty of their Enemies.
After the Rejoicing, all the Women apply'd
themselves to make ready their Provisions, some
to pound *Indian* Corn, others to boil Meal,
which they call *Grouller*, and others to bake
Bread, to carry to the Warriors. They all set
out the 19th to meet them, and we thought it
in Policy convenient to send Meat to our Men
which was done by the *French* Man of *Provence*,
who went with the Women.

That same Day, at Night, the Victorious Army return'd, and vve vvere inform'd, that their
Enemies, whom they call *Cannohatinno*, had
expected them boldly, but that having heard
the Noise, and felt the Effects of our Mens
Fire Arms, they all fled, so that the *Cenis* had
either kill'd or taken Forty Eight Men and
Women. They had slain several of the latter, who fled to the Tops of Trees, for want
of Time to make their Escape otherwise; so
that

Account
of the Bat-
tle fought
by the Ce-
nis.

that many more Women had periſh'd than Men.

Barbarity of the Men towards a Woman taken. They brought Home two of thoſe Women alive, one of whom had her Head flead for the Sake of her Hair and Skin. They gave that wretched Creature a Charge of Powder and a Ball, and ſent Her home; bidding her carry that Preſent to her Nation, and to aſſure them, they ſhould be again treated after the ſame Manner, that is, kill'd with Fire Arms.

of the Women. The other Woman was kept to fall a Sacrifice to the Rage and Vengeance of the Women and Maids; who having arm'd themſelves with thick Stakes, ſharp Pointed at the End, Conducted that Wretch to a By-Place, where each of thoſe Furies began to torment her, ſometimes with the Point of their Staff, and ſometimes laying on her with all their Might. One tore off her Hair, another cut off her Finger, and every one of thoſe outrageous Women endeavour'd to put her to ſome exquiſite Torture, to revenge the Death of their Husbands and Kinſmen, who had been kill'd in the former Wars; ſo that the unfortunate Creature expected her Death Stroke, as Mercy.

Inhumanity. At laſt, one of them gave her a Stroke with a heavy Club on the Head, and another run her Stake ſeveral Times into her Body, with which ſhe fell down Dead on the Spot. Then they cut that miſerable Victim into Morſels, and oblig'd ſome Slaves of that Nation, they had been long poſſeſs'd of to eat them.

Cruel Trophies. Thus our Warriors return'd Triumphant from that Expedition. They ſpar'd none of the Priſoners they had taken, except two little Boys, and brought Home all the Skins of their
Heads

Heads, with the Hair, to be kept as Trophies and glorious Memorials of their Victory.

The next Day all thofe Savages met in their Chief's Cottage, whether all the abovemention'd Heads of Hair were carry'd in State. Then they made extraordinary Rejoicings in that Cottage, whence they went to the Huts of the other Prime Men, to perform the fame Ceremony. This Rejoicing lafted three Days, our *French* Companions, who had been the Caufe of their Victory, being call'd to it, and highly entertain'd, after their Manner. It will not be difagreeable to the Reader, that I here particularly defcribe that Ceremony, which after having been perform'd in the Cottages of the Chief Men, was repeated in ours.

In the firft Place, the Cottage was made very clean, adorn'd, and abundant of Mats laid on the Floor, on which the Elders, and the moft confiderable Perfons fate ; after which, one of them, who is in the Nature of an Orator, or Mafter of the Ceremonies ftood up and made a Speech, of which we underftood not a Word. Soon after that Difcourfe was ended, the Warriors arriv'd, who had flain any in Battle, marching in their proper Order, each of them carrying a Bow and two Arrows, and before every one of them went his Wife, carrying the Enemies Head of Hair. Two little Boys, whofe Lives they had fpar'd, as has been faid before, one of them who was wounded being a Horfeback, clos'd the Proceffion ; at the Head whereof, was a Woman carrying a large Reed, or Cane in her Hand.

As they came up to the Orator, the Warrior took the Head of Hair his Wife had brought

Ceremony of Rejoicing

K

brought, and preſented it to him, which the ſaid Orator receiv'd with both his Hands, and after having held it out towards the four Quarters of the World, he laid it down on the Ground, and then took the next, performing the ſame Ceremony, till he had gone over them all.

When the Ceremony was ended, they ſerv'd up the *Sagamite*, in the Nature of Haſty Pudding, which thoſe Women had provided, and before any one touch'd it, the Maſter of the Ceremonies took ſome in a Veſſel, which he carry'd as an Offering to thoſe Heads of Hair. Then he lighted a Pipe of Tabacco, and blow'd the Smoke upon them. That being perform'd, they all fell to the Meat, *Bits of the Woman that had been ſacrific'd, were ſerv'd up to the two Boys of her Nation.* They alſo ſerv'd up dry'd Tongues of their Enemies, and the whole concluded with Dancing and Singing after their Manner: After which, they went to other Cottages to repeat the ſame Ceremony.

There was no Talk of our Deſign till thoſe Rejoycings were over, and I begn to conceive good Hopes of our Succeſs. The two Murderers, *Teiſſier* and *Larcheveque*, who had both a Hand in the Death of Monſr. *de la Sale*, had promis'd to go along with us, provided Monſr. *Cavelier* would pardon them, and he had given them his Word ſo to do. In this Expectation we continu'd till the 25th, when our French Men, who had been at the War, repair'd to our Cottage, and we conſulted about our Buſineſs.

Hiens

Hiens and others of his Gang, difapproving of our Defign, reprefented to us fuch Difficulties as they look'd upon to be unfurmountable, under which we muft inevitably perifh, or at leaft be oblig'd to return to the fame Place. *Hiens* told us, that for his own Part, he would not hazard his Life to return into *France*, only to have his Head chopp'd off, and perceiving we anfwer'd Nothing to that, but that we perfifted in our Refolution. *It is requifite then*, faid he, *to divide what Effects remain*.

Accordingly he laid afide, for F. *Anaftafius*, Meffieurs *Cavelier*, the Uncle and the Nephew, thirty Axes, four or five Dozens of Knives, about thirty Pounds of Powder and the like Quantity of Ball. He gave each of the others two Axes, two Knives, two or three Pounds of Powder, with as much Ball, and kept the reft. As for the Horfes, he kept the beft and left us the three leaft. Monfieur *Cavelier* ask'd him for fome Strings of Beads, which he granted, and feiz'd upon all the late Monfr. *de la Sale*'s Cloaths, Baggage and other Effects, befides above a thoufand Livres in Money, which belong'd to the late Monfr. *le Gros*, who dy'd at our Dwelling of St. *Lewis*. Before our Departure, it was a fenfible Affliction to us, to fee that Villain walk about, in a fcarlet Coat, with gold Galons, which had belong'd to the late Monfr. *de la Sale*, and which, as I have faid, he had feiz'd.

Hiens gives the others what he pleafes, and feizes the reft of the Effects.

After that, *Hiens* and his Companions withdrew to their own Cottage, and we refolv'd not to put off our Departure any longer. Accordingly, we made ready our Horfes, which much alarm'd the Natives, and efpecially the

Mr. Cavelier and his Company part from the others.

Chief

Chief of them, who ſaid and did all he cond to obſtruct our Journey, promiſing us Wives, Plenty of Proviſions, repreſenting to us the immenſe Dangers, as well from Enemies, who ſurrounded them, as from the bad and impaſſable Ways and the many Woods and Rivers we were to paſs. However, we were not to be moved, and only ask'd one Kindneſs of him, in obtaining of which, there were many Difficulties, and it was, that he would give us Guides to conduct us to *Cappa*; but at length, after much Trouble and many Promiſes of a good Reward, one was granted, and two others went along with him.

All Things being thus order'd for our Departure, we took Leave of our Hoſts, paſs'd by *Hiens*'s Cottage and embrac'd him and his Companions. We ask'd him for another Horſe, which he granted. He deſired an Atteſtation in *Latin* of Monſieur *Cavelier*, that he had not been concern'd in the Murder of Monſieur *de la Sale*, which was given him, becauſe there was *French* no refuſing of it; and we ſet forward without *Men ſtay* *Larcheveque* and *Meunier*, who did not keep their *with the* Word with us, but remain'd among thoſe Bar*Indians.* barians, being infatuated with that Courſe of Libertiniſm they had run themſelves into. Thus *Only ſeven* there were only ſeven of us that ſtuck together *ſet out for* to return to *Canada*, *viz.* Father *Anaſtaſius*, *Canada.* Meſſieurs *Cavelier* the Uncle and the Nephew, the Sieur *de Marle*, one *Teiſſier*, a young Man born at *Paris*, whoſe Name was *Bartholomew* and I, with ſix Horſes and the three *Indians*, who were to be our Guides; a very ſmall Number for ſo great an Enterprize, but we put ourſelves entirely into the Hands of Divine Providence,

con-

confiding in God's Mercy, which did not for- *May 1687*
fake us.

After the firſt Day's Journey we incamp'd
on the Bank of the River, we had left not long
before, lay there that Night, and the next Day,
cut down Trees to make a Sort of Bridge or
Planks to paſs over it; handing over our Goods
from one to another, and ſwimming over our
Horſes; which Work we were frequently o-
blig'd to repeat, and as often as we had afterwards Occaſion to paſs Rivers on our Way,
which we held on till the 29th, every Day
meeting with ſome Cottage, and at laſt, a Ham-
let or Village, into which we went, and the
Indian Inhabitants told us, they were call'd
Nahordikhe, and that they were Allies to the
Cenis.

We barter'd with them for ſome Proviſions,
and their Chief offer'd to go with us as far as
the *Aſſonys*, who were not farther off than about *Nahor-*
three Leagues, which he accordingly did; but *dikhesand*
it happening to rain when we came thither, *Aſſony*
and the *Aſſonys* having had no Notice before
hand, we found but indifferent Reception.

However, we were conducted to the Chief's
Cottage; the Elders had Notice given them,
they reſorted thither, and when our Horſes
were unloaded, and our Goods plac'd in a Corner of the Cottage, which the Chief had allotted us, we gave them to underſtand, that
our Intention was to go farther, to fetch Commodities to trade with them, at which they
were pleas'd. They gave us to eat, and the
Elders ſtay'd ſome Part of the Evening with us,
which made us ſomewhat Uneaſy, and oblig'd us

to

June 1687 to be upon our Guard; however the Night paſs'd without any Diſturbance.

The next Morning the Elders came to us again. They had provided Mats without the Cottage, and made Signs to us to go thither and ſit down upon them, as we did, leaving two of our Company to guard the Baggage. We repeated to them what we had ſaid the Night before, and made them ſome Preſents of Axes, Knives, Strings of Beads and Rings. They ſignify'd they were ſorry we would go away, and endeavour'd the beſt they could, to make us ſenſible of the ſame Obſtacles the others had ſignify'd to us; but it was all in Vain; however, vve ſtay'd till the firſt of *June*, all the vvhile bartering and gathering the beſt Stock of Proviſions vve could.

Good Entertainment

The Second, vve remov'd from that Cottage, vvhere vve had ſome Jealouſy, and vvent to another, a Quarter of a League from it, vvhere the Chief of it gave us a very good Reception, An old Woman, vvho vvas either his Mother, or Governeſs of the Cottage, took particular Care of us: We vvere firſt ſerv'd at eating, and to keep her in that good Mind, vve now and then made her ſome little Preſents, vvhilſt ſhe, by her Care and Kindneſs, ſpar'd our Proviſions, vvhich vvere neceſſary for our Journey.

A continual Rain oblig'd us to ſtay there till the 13th. During our Stay, the Natives made ſeveral Feaſts, to vvhich vve vvere always invited; and at length the Rain ceaſing, vve reſolv'd to ſet out, notwithſtanding all Monſieur *Cavelier* and the Prieſt's Apprehenſions, which we ſurmounted, and directed our

Courſe

Course towards the *N. E.* with two *Indians,* June 1687 who were to conduct us only a small Way, and who accordingly soon left us, whatsoever Promises we could make them. They departed to return Home, promising they would come to us again. We encamp'd that Night on the Bank of a Rivulet.

The 14th and 15th, we held on our Way, *Bad Ways.* frequently meeting with Sloughs, which very much fatigued us, because we were oblig'd to unload our Horses for them to pass, and prevent their sticking in the Mire and fat Soil, whence we could not have drawn them out, and consequently we were fain to carry all our Luggage on our ovvn Backs.

Whilst we halted about Noon, that our Horses might graze, as was usually done by us, we discover'd our two *Assony Indians* returning towards us, at which we were much rejoiced, because they had a better Notion than ourselves of the Way we were to go. We made them eat and smoke, and then set out again.

The 16th, we came to a great River, which we pass'd as we had done the first, and after that, met with very bad Ways.

The 17th, one of our Company being indispos'd, we could not set out till Noon, and held on till the 21st, crossing several Sloughs and Rivers, and then one of our *Indians* being out of Order, it oblig'd us to stay on the Bank of a River we had pass'd. The other *Indian* seeing his Comrade sick, went a Hunting, and brought a wild Goat; for there are many in that Country. The *Indians* have the Art of dressing the Heads of those Creatures, which they put upon

their

June 1687 their own, and imitate them fo exactly, that
they can come very near to them, and then
Art to kill feldom fail of killing. The fame Method they
Goats and ufe for Turkeys and other wild Fowl, and fo
Wild Fowl. draw them clofe to themfelves.

The 22d, our *Indian* being fomewhat recover'd
we decamp'd and proceeded along a better
Way and pleafanter Country, than that we had
left behind, and as we enquir'd the beft we could
of thofe our *Indians*, concerning the Neighbouring Nations and thofe we were going towards,
among others they nam'd to us, that they call'd
Cappa. M. *Cavelier* told us, he remember'd he had
heard his late Brother Monfieur *de la Sale* name
that Nation, and fay he had feen it as he vvent
from *Canada* towards the *Miffifipi*. This put
us in Hopes, that vve fhould fucceed in our Difcovery.

Fine Mea- The 23d, being near a Village, we had been
dows. in Search of, one of our *Indians* went before, to
give Notice of our Arrival. In the mean Time
vve crofs'd moft lovely Plains and Meadows,
border'd with fine Groves of beautiful Trees,
vvhere the Grafs vvas fo high, that it hinder'd
our Horfes going, and vve vvere oblig'd to
clear the Paffage for them.

When we were within Half a League of the
Village, we faw an *Indian*, mounted on a large
grey Mare, coming along vvith our Native,
to meet us, and were told, that Horfeman
vvas the Chief of the Village, attended by fome
others of the fame Place. As foon as that Chief
came up to us, he exprefs'd very much Kindnefs
and Affection ; vve gave him to underftand, that
vve did no Body any Harm, unlefs we were firft
attack'd. Then we made him fmoke, and when
that

that vvas done, he made Signs to us to follow
him, vvhich vve did, till we came to the Bank
of a River, where he again defir'd us to ftay,
whilft he vvent to give Notice to the Elders.

Soon after, a Number of them came, and ha- *M. Cave-*
ving join'd us, fignify'd, that they vvere come *lier and*
to carry us to their Village. Our *Indians* made *the reft*
Signs, that it was the Cuftom of the Country, *carry'd on*
and we muft fubmit, and let them do as they *the Backs*
thought fit. Tho' we were much out of Counte- *of Indians.*
nance at that Ceremony, feven of the prime
Men among them would have us mount on their
Backs or Shoulders. Monfieur *Cavelier* being
our Chief, mounted firft, and then the reft did
the fame.

As for my own Part, being of a pretty large
Size and loaded vvith Cloaths, a Firelock, a
Cafe of Piftols, Powder and Ball, a Kettle and
other Implements, there is no Doubt but I made
a fufficient Burden for him that carry'd me, and
becaufe I was taller than he and my Feet would
have hung upon the Ground, two other *Indians*
held them up for me ; fo that I had three to
carry me. Other *Indians* took hold of our
Horfes to lead them, and in that ridiculous E-
quipage we arriv'd at the Village. Our Carriers,
who had gone a long Quarter of a League, had
need enough to reft, and we to be fet down,
that we might laugh in private, for it behov'd
us to take Care not to do it before them.

As foon as we were come to the Chief's Cot- *Ceremo-*
tage, where we found above two hundred Per- *nies at*
fons, who were come to fee us, and that our *their Re-*
Horfes were unloaded, the Elders gave us to *ception.*
underftand, that it was their Cuftom to wafh
                              Strangers

Strangers at their firſt Coming ; but that we being clad, they would only waſh our Faces ;
which one of thoſe Elders did, with fair Water
they had in a Sort of Earthen Veſſel, and he
only waſh'd our Forehead.

Speeches made to them. After this ſecond Ceremony, the Chief made
Signs to us, to ſit down on a Sort of little Scaf-
fold, rais'd about 4 Foot above the Ground, and
made of Wood and Canes, where when we were
plac'd, the Chiefs of the Villages being four in
Number, came and made Speeches to us, one
after another. We liſtned to them with Patience, tho' we underſtood not one Word of
what they ſaid to us ; being tir'd with the
Length of their Harangues, and much more
with the violent Heat of the Sun, which was
juſt over our Heads.

When the Speeches were ended, the Purport
whereof, as near as we could gueſs, was only to
aſſure us, that we were very welcome ; we gave
them to underſtand, that vve vvere going into
our own Country, deſigning to return ſpeedily,
to bring them ſeveral Sorts of Commodities and
ſuch Things as they ſhould ſtand in need
of.

Next, we made them the uſual Preſents of
Axes, Knives, Strings of Beads, Needles and
Pins, for their Wives, telling them, that
when we return'd we would give them
more.

Their En-tertain-ment. We farther ſignify'd to them, that if they
would afford us ſome Corn or Meal, we would
give them other Things in Exchange, which
they agreed to. After this they made us eat
Sagamite, or Haſty-pudding, Bread, Beans, Pompions and other Things, which we had ſufficient
Need

Need of. Most of us having scarce eaten any Thing all that Day, some for Want, and others out of Devotion, as Monsr. *Cavelier*, who would observe the Fast of St. *John Baptist*'s Eve, whose Name he bore. It is to be observ'd, that the Pompions are incomparably better there, than with us.

The 24th, the Elders met again in our Cottage. We gave them to understand, they would oblige us, in furnishing Guides to conduct us to the Village of *Cappa*, which was in our Way ; but instead of granting it, they earnestly intreated us, to stay with them and go to the Wars against their Enemies, having been told Wonders of our Firelocks, which we promis'd to do when we return'd, and that it should be shortly, and they seem'd to rest satisfy'd.

Thus our Hopes increas'd, but the Joy it occasion'd was allay'd by a dismal Accident that befell us. Monsieur *de Marle*, one of the prime Men of our Company, having Breakfasted, would needs go Bath himself in the River we had pass'd the Day before, and not knowing how to swim, he went too far and step'd into a Hole, whence he could not recover himself, but was unfortunately drowned. Young Monsieur *Cavelier*, having been told that Monsieur *de Marle* was going to Bath himself, ran after him, and coming to the River, saw he was drowning, he ran back to acquaint us: We hasted thither with a Number of *Indians*, who were there before us ; but all too late, some of them div'd, and brought him up dead from the Bottom of the Water.

Mr. de Marle *drown'd.*

We

His Funeral.

We carry'd him to the Cottage, ſhedding many Tears, the *Indians* bore Part in our Sorrow, and we paid him the laſt Duties, offering up the uſual Prayers; after which he was buried in a ſmall Field, behind the Cottage; and whereas, during that doleful Ceremony, we pray'd, reading in our Books, particularly Monſieur *Cavelier*, the Prieſt and Father *Anaſtaſius*, the *Indians* gaz'd on us with Amazement, becauſe we talk'd, looking upon the Leaves, and we endeavour'd to give them to underſtand, that we pray'd to God for the dead Man, pointing up to Heaven.

Humanity of the Indians.

We muſt do this Right to thoſe good People, as to declare, that they expreſs'd ſingular Humanity upon that doleful Accident, as appear'd by the ſenſible Teſtimony of their Actions, and all the Methods they us'd to let us underſtand how great a Share they bore in our Sorrow; which we ſhould not have found in ſeveral Parts of *Europe*.

During our ſhort Stay in that Place, we obſerv'd a Ceremony that was perform'd by the Chief's Wife, *viz*. that every Morning ſhe

Indian Ceremony to the Dead.

went to Monſieur *de Marle*'s Grave, and carry'd a little Basket of parch'd Ears of Corn to lay on it, the meaning whereof we could not underſtand. Before our Departure, we were inform'd, that the Villages belonging to our Hoſts, being four in Number, all ally'd together were call'd, *Aſſony, Nathoſos, Nachitos* and *Cadodaquio.*

Indian Nations.

On the 27th, having been inform'd by the Natives, that we ſhould find Canoes, to paſs a River that was on our Way. Father *Anaſtaſius* and I went to ſee whether, what they told us

was

was true. We found that River was a Branch *June* 1687
of the same we had already pass'd, the Channel
of it being pleasant and navigable, and saw
some Canoes, in one of which the *Indians* carry'd us over to the other Side, whether we went
to see what convenient Place there was for our
Horses to come ashore. We found a very
proper Place, and returning, made our Report
to Monsieur *Cavelier*, who being then much out
of Order with Pains in his Feet, we were oblig'd to stay there, till the 30th.

During that Time, vve vvere frequently vi- *Janiquo*
sited by the *Indians*, both Old and Young, and *Nation.*
of both Sexes, and even the Chiefs of the Nation, call'd *Janiquo*, came to see us, and with
them we often convers'd in dumb Show, and e-
very Evening the Women, attended by the Warriors, with their Bows and Arrows, resorted to *Doleful*
our Cottage, to sing a doleful Sort of Song, *Entertain-*
shedding Tears at the same Time. This would *ment.*
have given us some Uneasiness, had we not
before seen the same Ceremony, and been inform'd, that those Women repair in that Manner to the Chief's Cottage, to intreat him, singing and weeping, to take Revenge on those,
who have kill'd their Husbands, or Relations,
in former Wars, as I have observ'd before. In
all other Respects, the Manners and Customs of
this Nation, being much the same as those of
the *Cenis*, I shall add no more concerning
them.

The 29th, at Night, we gave Notice to the
Chief, that we would set out the next Day, vve
made him some Presents in particular, and the
like to his Wife, because she had taken special
Care of us, and departed on the 30th. The
Chief,

Chief, attended by many other *Indians*, whom we found in the Cottages on our Way, vvent to Conduct us as far as the River, which we cross'd in Canoes, and swam over our Horses. There we took Leave of our Conductors, to whom we gave some Strings of Beads for their Wives, and their Chief would needs Conduct us to the next Village.

By the Way we came to a Cottage, where our Guide made us halt, and there they gave Cadoda- us to eat. Then we held on our Journey to a quio *Vil.* Village call'd *Cadodaquio*, and were conducted *lage.* to the Chief's Cottage, who receiv'd us courteously, being a Friend to him that went with us. It was requisite to unload our Horses to lie there, and we signified to the Chief, that we stood in Need of Provisions. He spoke to the Women, who brought us some Meal, which we purchased with Strings of Beads, and the Chief, who conducted us thither, took his Leave.

Having no Design to stay there any Time, we had desired the Chief to appoint some Person to guide us to the Village call'd *Cahainihoua*, which was in our Way. It happen'd by good Fortune, that there were then in that Place some Men and Women of the said Village, who who were come to fetch some Wood, fit to make Bows, there being Plenty of that Sort of Trees they make them of, about the Village we were in. We signify'd our Design to them and they gave us to understand they would be glad to bear us Company. In the Conversation we had with them, they made us comprehend, that they had seen People like us, who had Firelocks and a House, and that they were acquainted with the *Cappa's*, which was very pleasing to us.

Because

Becaufe they were not to depart till two Days *June* 1687. after, we refolv'd to ftay for them.

We obferv'd, that there was a Difference between the Language of thofe People and the Inhabitants of the Village we vvere in, from that of the *Cenis*, and that they had fome peculiar Ceremonies, one whereof is, that vvhen the Women have their Terms, they leave the Company of their Husbands and vvithdraw into other Cottages appointed for that Purpofe, vvhich no Perfon is to come near, upon Pain of being reputed unclean.

Peculiar Cuftom.

Thofe Women have their Faces ftill more disfigur'd, than the others we had feen before ; for they make feveral Streaks, or Scores on them, whereas the others had but one. They adorn themfelves with little Locks of fine red Hair ; which they make faft to their Ears, in the Nature of Pendants. In other Refpects they are not difagreeable, and neither Women nor Maids are fo ill-natur'd as to make their Lovers pine for them. They are not difficult of Accefs, and they foon make a Return for a fmall Prefent.

Ornaments of Women.

The Men wear their Hair fhort, like our *Capucins*, they anoint it with a Sort of Oyl, or Greafe, and curl it like Snails, after which they ftrew on it a Sort of Down, or Lint, died red, as we do Powder, which is done when they defign to be very fine, in order to appear in their Affemblies. They are very fond of their Children, and all the Way of chaftifing them they ufe, is to throw Water at them, without ever beating or giving them ill Words.

The Men.

The

The *Indians* that were of the Village of *Co-hainihoua* and to conduct us thither, not being ready to ſet out on *Wedneſday* the 2d of *July*, as they had promis'd, a young *Indian* offer'd himſelf, ſaying, he would conduct us ſafe thither, and we ſet out with him, ſtill directing our Courſe towards the *N. E.* We kept cloſe along the ſame River we had croſs'd, and found it very pleaſant and navigable, the Banks of it cover'd with fine Trees of ſeveral Sorts.

We had not travell'd above a League, before our Guide gave us to underſtand, that he had forgot a Piece of hard dry'd Skin he had to make him Shoes, which he would go fetch and return to us, pointing to us with his Hand, which Way we were to go, and telling us we ſhould ſoon come to a River.

This ſudden Change in the *Indian* was ſomewhat ſurprizing and very much perplex'd us ; however we held on our Way, and ſoon came to the River he had mention'd to us, which was very pleaſant and deep. We croſs'd it the next Day, on a Sort of Float, which we made with much Toil and Labour, and our Horſes ſwam over. Some Time after we were paſſed, we ſaw the *Indians* coming, who had promiſed to bear us Company, and were glad to find our Float, to croſs the ſame River, as they did, and proceeded on our Journey all together.

The 4th, 5th and 6th, we did the ſame, croſſing a very fine Country, but water'd by many Brooks, Streams and Rivers. We found Abundance of wild Goats, Turkeys and other wild Fowl, whereof our *Indians* kill'd many.

Plenty of Game.

On the 6th, whilſt we halted on the Bank of a River to eat, we heard the Tingling of ſome
ſmall

them in a Circle, and joyning the Tops together, from the Dome, or round Top, then
they laſh and cover them with Weeds. When
they remove their Dwellings, they generally
burn the Cottages they leave, and build new
on the Ground they deſign to inhabit.

Their Moveables are ſome Bullocks Hides *Their move*
and Goats Skins well cur'd, ſome Mats cloſe *ables.*
wove, wherewith they adorn their Huts, and
ſome Earthen Veſſels, which they are very
skilful at making, and wherein they boil their
Fleſh or Roots, or *Sagamiſe*, which, as has been
ſaid, is their Pottage. They have alſo ſome
ſmall Baskets made of Canes, ſerving to put in
their Fruit and other Proviſions. Their Beds
are made of Canes, rais'd two or three Foot
above the Ground, handſomly fitted with Mats *Beds.*
and Bullocks Hides, or Goats Skins well cur'd,
which ſerve them for Feather Beds, or Quilts
and Blankets ; and thoſe Beds are parted one
from another by Mats hung up.

When they deſign to Till the Ground, they
give one another Notice, and very often above *Tillage.*
an Hundred of each Sex meet together. When
they have till'd that Piece of Land, after their
Manner, and ſpent part of the Day, thoſe the
Land belongs to, give the others to Eat, and
then they ſpend the reſt of the Day in Dancing
and Merry Making. This ſame is practis'd
from Canton to Canton, and ſo they till
Land all together.

This Tillage conſiſts in breaking up juſt the *Inſtrument*
Surface of the Earth with a Sort of Wooden *for Tilling.*
Inſtrument, like a little Pick-axe, which they
make by ſplitting the End of a thick Piece of
Wood, that ſerves for a Handle, and putting
another

Mar.1687 another Piece of Wood ſharp Pointed at one
End into the Slit. This Inſtrument ſerves
them inſtead of a Hoe, or Spade, for they have
no Iron Tools. When the Land has been thus
Women ſow till'd or broke up, the Women Sow and Plant
the *Indian* Corn, Beans, Pompions, Water
Melons, and other Grain and Garden Ware,
which is for their Suſtenance.

The *Indians* are generally Handſom, but
Indians disfigure themſelves by making Scores, or
disfigure Streaks on their Faces, from the Top of the
themſelves. Forehead down the Noſe to the Tip of the
Chin; which is done by pricking the Skin with
Needles, or other ſharp Inſtruments, till it
bleeds, whereon they ſtrevv fine Powder of
Charcoal, and that ſinks in and mixes with the
Blood within the Skin. They alſo make after
the ſame Manner, the Figures of living Creatures, of Leaves and Flowers on their Shoulders, Thighs, and other Parts of their Bodies,
and Paint themſelves, as has been ſaid before,
with Black or Red, and ſometimes both together.

The Women are generally well Shap'd, and
Women, would not be diſagreeable, did they adhere
to Nature; but they Diſguiſe themſelves as
ridiculouſly as the Men, not only with the
Streak they have like them down their
Face, but by other Figures they make on it,
at the Corners of their Eyes, and on the other
Parts of their Bodies; whereof they make
more particular Show on their Boſom, and
thoſe who have the moſt, are reckoned the
handſomeſt; tho' that pricking in that Part be
extremely painful to them.

It is they that do all the Work in the Cottage, either in Pounding the *Indian* Corn and Baking the Meal, or making the Pottage of the said Meal, by them call'd *Sagamite*, or in dressing their other Provisions, or drying or parching, or smoaking their Flesh, fetching the Wood they have Occasion for, or the Flesh of Bullocks, or other Beasts kill'd by their Husbands in the Woods, which are often at a great Distance, and afterwards Dressing them as has been said. They Sow and Plant, when the Land has been broke up, and in short, do almost all that is requisite for the Support of Life.

Mar. 1687
They do the Work at Home.

I did not observe that those Women were naturally given to Lewdness ; but their Virtue is not Proof against some of our Toys, when presented them, as Needles, Knives, and more particularly Strings of Beads, whereof they make Necklaces and Bracelets, and that Temptation is rarely resisted by them, and the less because they have no Religion or Law to prohibit that vile Practice. It is true their Husbands, when they take them in the Fact, sometimes do punish them, either by Separation or otherwise ; but that is rare.

Their Behaviour.

The Country of those *Indians* being generally subject to no Cold, almost all of them go naked ; unless when the *North* Wind blows, then they cover themselves with a Bullock's Hide, or Goat's Skin cur'd. The Women wear nothing but a Skin, Mat, or Clout, hanging round them like a Petticoat, and reaching down half way their Legs, which hides their Nakedness before and behind. On their Heads they have nothing

Habit.

thing but their Hair platted and knotted behind.

Manners. As for their Manners, it may be said of these as of all other *Indians* of that great Continent, that they are not Mischievous, unless wrong'd or attack'd ; in which Case they are all Fierce and Revengeful. They watch all Opportunities to be Reveng'd, and never let any slip, when offer'd, which is the Cause of their being continually at War with their Neighbours, and of that Martial Humour, so Predominant among them.

Religion. As to the Knowledge of a God, they did not seem to us to have any fix'd Notion of Him; it is true, we met with some on our Way, who as far as we could judge, believ'd, there was some Superior Being, which was above all Things, and this they testify'd by lifting up their Hands and Eyes to Heaven, yet without any Manner of Concern, as believing that the said exalted Being does not regard at all, what is done here below. However none of them having any Places of Worship, Ceremonies, or Prayers, to denote the divine Homage, it may be said of them all, that they have no Religion, at least those that we saw.

Ceremonies. However, they observe some Ceremonies ; but whether they have any Regard to a real or pretended Superior Being, or whether they are only popular, and proceeding from Custom, is what we were not able to discover. Those Ceremonies are as follows. When the Corn is ripe, they gather a certain Quantity in a Maund or Basket, which is placed on a Sort of Seat or Stool, dedicated to that Use, and serving only upon those misterious Occasions, which they have a great Veneration for. The

The Basket with the Corn being placed on that honour'd Stool, one of the Elders holds out his Hands over it, and talks a long Time; after which, the said old Man diftributes the Corn among the Women, and no Perfon is allow'd to eat of the new Corn, till eight Days after that Ceremony. This feems to be in the Nature of Offering up or Blefling the firft Fruits of their Harveft.

At their Affemblies, when the *Sagamite*, or Pottage, which is the moft effential Part of their Meal, is boil'd in a great Pot, they place that Pot on the Stool of Ceremony above mention'd, and one of the Elders ftretches out his Hands over it, muttering fome Words between his Teeth for a confiderable Time, after which, they fall to eat.

When the young Folks are grown up to be fit to go to the Wars, and take upon them to be Soldiers, their Garment, confifting of fome Skin, or Clout, together with their Bow, Quiver and Arrows, is placed on the aforefaid Stool, an old Man ftretches out his Hands over them, mutters the Words as above, and then the Garments, Bows, Quivers, and Arrows are given to the Perfons they belong to. This may be compar'd to Something of a Ceremony of Knighting among them. The fame Ceremonies are us'd by them in the cultivating of their Grain and Product, but particularly of the Tabacco, whereof they have a Sort, which has fmaller Leaves than Ours; it is almoft ever green, and they ufe it in Leaves.

This is what we obferv'd among the *Cenis*, whofe Cuftoms and Manners differ very little from thofe of other Nations, which we had feen

before,

Mar. 1687 before and faw afterwards. As to the Point of
Religion, it is not to be infer'd from what I
have faid above, that there is none throughout
that vaſt Continent : The Account I have given
only regards thoſe Nations we faw ; there may
be others that have ſome Worſhip, and I remember I have heard Monſieur *de la Sale* fay,
that the Nation call'd *Takenſa*, neighbouring
on the *Iſlinois*, ador'd the Fire, and that they
had Cottages which they made uſe of, as Temples.

Nation,
what is
meant
here by it. Before I conclude this ſhort Account of the
Religion, Cuſtoms and Manners of the *Cenis,*
which belong'd properly to this Place, it is
fit here alfo to obſerve, that the Word
Nation, is not to be underſtood, among thoſe
Indians, to denote a People poſſeſſing a whole
Province, or vaſt Extent of Land. Thoſe Nations are no other than a Parcel of Villages,
diſpers'd for the Space of twenty or thirty
Leagues at moſt, which compoſe a diſtinct People or Nation ; and they differ from one another rather in Language than in Manners,
wherein they are all much alike, or at leaſt
they vary but little, as has been mention'd
above. As for the Names of them, here follow thoſe of ſuch as we travel'd through, or
were near the Way we held from our leaving
our Habitation near the Bay of the Holy Ghoſt,
till we came among the *Cenis.*

Names of
Nations. The *Spicheats, Kabayes, Thecamons, Thearemets,*
Kiabaha, Chaumenes, Kouans, Arhau, Enepiahe,
Ahonerhopiheim, Koienkahe, Konkone, Omeaoſſe,
Keremen, Ahekouen, Meghty, Tetamenes, Otenmar-
hen, Kouayon and *Meracouman.* All theſe Na-
tions are on the North of the River called *la*
Maligne.

Maligne. Thofe that follow, are on the Weft
and North-Weft of the fame River.

The *Kannehouan, Tohaha, Pihir, Cagabegux, Onapien, Pickar, Tokau, Kuaffes, Chancres, Teferabocretes, Tfepehouen, Fercouteha, Panego, Petao, Petzare, Peifacho, Peihoun, Orcan* and *Piou.* This laft Nation borders upon the *Cenis,* at the Entrance into whofe firft Village I left my Reader, to give an Account of the Inhabitants, and thither I return, to proceed with my Relation and our Journey to the Village, the *French Man* who liv'd among the Natives was to conduct us to.

We arriv'd there at Night, and found other Elders coming out to meet us, much after the fame Manner as the others mention'd before. They led us to their Cottage, made us fit down on Mats and fmoke, but not with fo much Ceremony as the others. That done, it was Time for us to take our Reft, having given them to underftand that we were weary.

The *French Provencal* would needs have us go to his Cottage, that is to the Hut where he French had his Dwelling ; for, as I have faid, there *Entertain-*are feveral Families in one of them, and that *ed by the*was one of the greateft in the Canton, having *Natives.*been the Habitation of one of their Chief's, lately deceafed.

They allotted us a Place there, for our Goods and Packs, the Women immediately made *Sagamite* or Pottage, and gave it us.   Having eaten, we afk'd the *French* Man whether we were fafe, and he anfwering we were, we lay down, but yet could not fleep found.

The next Day, being the firft of *April,* the Elders came to receive and conducted us to the Cottage where we had been the Day before.

After the uſual Ceremonies, we traded with them for Corn, Meal and Beans, giving in Exchange for the ſame, Needles, Knives, Rings *A Horſe* and other Toys. We alſo purchaſed a very *ſold for an* fine Stone Horſe, that would have been worth *Ax.* twenty Piſtoles in *France*, for an Ax.

The Day was ſpent in drivîng our ſmall Bargains and gathering Proviſions, which the Women brought. When that was done, it was agreed, that I ſhould remain there, to lay up more Store, and that the others ſhould return to our Company, which we had left near the River, to carry the Proviſions and ſatisfy them they might come ſafely.

Tho' I thought my ſelf not over ſecure among the *Indians*, and beſides had the Diſſatisfaĉtion of underſtanding none of their Language ; yet was I not unwilling to ſtay, that I might have an Opportunity of ſeeing the two other *French* Men, who had forſaken the late Monſieur *de la Sale*, when he firſt travell'd into that Country, that I might enquire of them, whether they had heard no talk of the *Miſſiſipi* River, for I ſtill held my Reſolution of parting from our wicked Murderers.

As ſoon as they were gone, I gave a young *Indian* a Knife, to go bid thoſe two other *French* Men come to me, and whilſt he was going I drove on my little Trade for Proviſions, and had frequent Viſits from the Elders, who entertain'd me by Signs, with an Account of their intended War ; to which I ſtill anſwer'd, nodding my Head, tho' very often I knew not what they meant. It was ſome Difficulty to me to ſecure my ſmall Merchandize, eſpecially at Night, for the Natives were covetous of them.

This

This Care, which kept me from Sleeping found, was the Occasion, that one Night I heard some Body moving near my Bed, and opening my Eyes, by the Light of the Fire, which never goes out in those Cottages, perceiv'd a Man stark naked, with a Bow and two Arrows *The Author* in his Hand, who came and sat down by me, *meets ano-* without saying any Thing. I view'd him for *ther French* some Time, I spoke to him, he made me no An- *Manamong* swer, and not knowing what to think of it, I *the Indians* laid hold of my two Pistols and my Firelock, which the Man perceiving, he went and sat by the Fire. I follow'd, and looking stedfastly on him, he knew and spoke to me, throwing his Arms about and embracing me, and then made himself known to be one of the French Men I had sent for.

We fell into Discourse, I ask'd him for his Comrade, he told me, he durst not come, for Fear of Monsieur *de la Sale.* They were both Sailors, this Man, who was of *Britany*, was call'd *Buter* ; the other, of *Rochelle, Grollet.* They had, in that short Space of Time, so perfectly enur'd themselves to the Customs of the Natives, *French* that they were become meer Savages. They *turn'd fa-* were naked, their Faces and Bodies with Fi- *vige.* gures wrought on them, like the rest. They had taken several Wives, been at the Wars and kill'd their Enemies with their Firelocks, which had gain'd them Reputation; but having no more Powder nor Ball, their Arms were grown useless, and they had been forc'd to learn to shoot with Bows and Arrows. As for Religion, they were not troubled with much of it, and that Libertine Life they led, was pleasing to them.

I acquainted this Man with the unfortunate Death of Monsr. *de la Sale,* his Nephew and the rest, at which, he was surpris'd and concern'd, at least in outward Appearance. I ask'd him, whether he had not heard talk of the *Missisipi* ; he told me he had not ; but only that there was a great River forty Leagues from thence towards the *N.W.* where the Natives said there were many Nations along its Banks. That made me believe, it was the very River we were in Search of, or at least that it must be the Way to come at it. I gave him to eat, and we went to Rest.

The next and the following Days, I continu'd trading, and the Elders their Visits, and their Discourse by Signs, concerning their intended War. Some of them gave me to understand, that they had been among the *Spaniards,* who are nevertheless about two hundred Leagues from them. They spoke some Words of broken *Spanish,* as *Capita,* instead of *Capitan,* a Captain, and *Cohavillo* instead of *Cavallo,* a Horse, and so of some others. *Buter,* the *French* Man return'd to his Dwelling, I gave him some Strings of Beads for his Wives, and desir'd him to send the other *French* Man to me.

In the mean Time my being alone, as to any Person I could converse with, grew very irksome to me, and I know not whether an old Man did not perceive it ; for he thought it would be proper to bring a Companion, to divert me, and at Night I was surpris'd to see a young Maid come sit down by me, and to hear the old Man tell me, he had brought her to be my Wife, and gave her to me ; but I had far different Thoughts to disturb me. I spoke not one

Indian Maid brought to the Author.

one Word to that poor Maid; she stay'd some
Time expecting I would take Notice of her, and
perceiving I did not stir, or speak one Word,
she withdrew.

Thus I continu'd, without hearing any News,
till the Sixth of *April*, when the two *French* Men,
I have spoken of, came both, in the *Indian*
Dress, each of them having only a Clout about
him, some Turky Feathers on their Shoulders,
their Heads and Feet bare. The latter of them
whose Name was *Grollet*, had not consented to
have his Face mark'd like the other, nor to
cut his Hair after the *Indian* Manner; for those
People cut off all theirs, except a small Lock
on the Crown of the Head, like the Turks,
only some of them have small Tresses on the
Temples.

I repeated to them the Narrative of Monsieur *de la Sale*'s unfortunate Story. They confirm'd what I had been told before, that the
Natives had talk'd to them of the great River,
which was forty Leagues off, towards the N. E.
and that there were People like us, that dwelt
on the Banks of it. This confirm'd me in the
Opinion, that it was the River so much sought
after, and that we must go that Way to return
to *Canada* or towards *New England*. They
told me, they would willingly go with us. I
desired them to keep it secret, which they did
not, for being inform'd that Monsieur *Cavelier*
and the others were coming, they went to meet
them, and I was again left alone.

The 8th, three Men came to me, one of
which was the *French* Man of *Provence*, with
each of them a Horse, sent by our People to
carry away all the Provisions I had got together,

I 4   having

having taken a Refolution, as thofe Perfons they had fent told us, to return to the Dwelling of St. *Lewis*, about the Bay of the fame Name, from whence we came; defigning, as they pretended, to build a Boat there, to carry them over to the Iflands of *America*; an impracticable Notion, for all our Carpenters were dead, and tho' they had been alive, they were fo ignorant, that none of them would have known which Way to go about that Work; befides that, we were deftitute of all Neceffaries for that Effect. However we muft obey, and fet out with our Provifions. The Rain having detain'd us the 9th on the Way, we could not come up to them till the next Day, being the Tenth.

Father *Anaftafius* gave me the Confirmation of that Defign, and farther told me how roughly they had been treated by thofe Murderers fince my Departure. I know not what it was that mov'd them to it, but they had refolved to feperate themfelves from thofe Villains, and that we fhould eat apart, *viz.* Monfieur *Cavelier* the Prieft, F. *Anaftafius*, young *Cavelier* and I, which was very agreeable to us, becaufe at leaft we could talk freely, which we durft not do before; but at the fame Time they allow'd us no more Provifions than would fuffice to keep us from ftarving, without giving us Share of any Flefh, tho' they often kill'd.

Our Tyrants ftill holding their Refolution to return to our former Habitation, thought they had not Horfes enough, and therefore deputed four of their Number, one of which was the *French* Man half turn'd *Indian*, to return to the Village of the *Cenis* and endeavour to barter for
some

some. At the same Time we agreed together *Apr.* 1687 to let those Gentlemen know, that we were too much fatigued to return with them to the said Habitation, and were resolved to remain in the Village of the *Cenis*. Monsieur *Cavelier* undertook to be our Speaker, and to desire *Duhaut*, who was Master of all, to give us some Axes, Knives and Strings of Beads, Powder and Shot, offering to give him a Note of his Hand for the same.

To conclude, Monsieur *Cavelier* made the Proposal to *Duhaut*, disguis'd it the best he was able, and *Duhaut* took till the next Day to return his Answer. He consulted with his Companions, and acquainted us, that they would deal handsomely by us, and give us half the Effects and all the Axes, intending to make the most Speed they could, to get to our former Dwelling, and to put in Execution what they had before design'd, as to the Building of a Bark. But in Case they could not succeed, for want of Necessaries, they would immediately return to us and bring F. *Zenobius* along with them, who would be serviceable to us, because, having been with Monsieur *de la Sale* upon his first Discovery, he understood the Language of the Nations about the *Missisipi* River. That whilst they were upon that Journey, we should take Care to gather a Stock of Provisions, and that if they succeeded in building the Bark, they would send us Word, that we might repair to them. Monsieur *Cavelier* approv'd of all they said, tho' we had other Designs. However it prov'd we were all Mistaken, for Providence had order'd Affairs otherwise.

Design of the Murderers.

We

We stay'd there some Time, expecting those who were gone to the *Cenis*, they staying longer than was requisite for that Journey. The overflowing of the River was their Pretence, but the true Reason was the Women, who as I have said, are not so forward as to offer themselves, but on the other Hand will not be over difficult in complying for some little Present, and those who were sent did not grudge their Time. In the mean while the Posture of our Affairs changed, as follows.

Murderers change their Mind. One of our half Savage *French* Men, whom I had acquainted with our Design to go find the *Missisipi*, communicated it to *Hautot*, telling him all the Particulars he had before acquainted me with ; whereupon *Duhaut* chang'd his Mind, as to the Design of going to the Habitation of St. *Lewis*, resolving to follow our intended Way and execute our Project. He imparted his Thoughts to his Companions, who were of the same Opinion, and all of them acquainted us, that they were ready to put in Execution the Enterprize we had form'd.

This Change troubled us very much, there being nothing we coveted more than to part with those Miscreants, from whom we could at a long Run expect no better Usage than they had afforded our Commander and his Friends. However, it was still requisite to dissemble, there being no other Remedy at that Time : But God's Justice provided for and rescued us. We continued in that Camp all the remaining Part of *April*, expecting the Persons that had been sent to the *Cenis*, and *Duhaut* intending to begin to put in Execution his Design of going to find out the *Missisipi*, with us, made

us

us advance towards the River that was near, in *May* 1687.
order to pass it as soon as fallen, and repair to
the Village of the *Cenis*.

We staid three Days longer in that Post, at *Murderers*
the End whereof, he we call'd *Larcheveque*, one *differ in*
of those that had been sent out, cross'd the *Opinion.*
River. He was *Duhaut*'s Creature, and an Accomplice in the Murder of Monsieur *de la Sale.*
He inform'd *Duhaut*, that one they call'd *Hiens*,
who was also one of our Messengers, and had
stay'd on the other Side of the River, had
heard of *Duhaut* and the rest altering their Resolution, and that he was not of their Mind
Hiens was a *Buccanier*, and by Birth a *German.*
Monsieur *de la Sale* had brought him from *Petit
Gouave*, and he was also accessary to the late
Murders.

After we had been some Days longer in the
same Place, *Hiens* arriv'd with the two half
Savage *French* Men and about twenty Natives.
He went immediately to *Duhaut*, and after
some Discourse, told him, he was not for going towards the *Missisipi*, because it would be of
dangerous Consequence for them, and therefore
demanded his Share of the Effects he had seiz'd
upon. *Duhaut* refusing to comply, and affirming, that all the Axes were his own; *Hiens*,
who it is likely had laid the Design before to
kill him, immediately drew his Pistol, and fired *Hiens*
it upon *Duhaut*, who stagger'd about four Paces *kills Du-*
from the Place and fell down dead. At the *haut, and*
same Time *Ruter*, who had been with *Hiens*, *Ruter*
fired his Piece upon *Liotot*, the Surgeon, and *Liotot.*
shot him thro' with three Balls.

These Murders committed before us, put me
into a terrible Consternation; for believing the
same

same was defign'd for me, I laid hold of my Fire-Lock to defend my felf ; but *Hiens* cry'd out to me, to fear nothing, to lay down my Arms, and affur'd me he had no Defign againft me; but that he had reveng'd his Mafter's Death. He alfo fatisfy'd Monfieur *Cavelier* and Father *Anaftafius*, who were as much frighted as my felf, declaring he meant them no Harm, and that tho' he had been in the Confpiracy, yet had he been prefent at the Time when Monfieur *de la Sale* was kill'd, he would not have confented, but rather have obftructed it.

Liotot liv'd fome Hours after, and had the good Fortune to make his Confeffion ; after which, the fame *Ruter*, put him out of his Pain, with a Piftol-Shot. We dug a Hole in the Earth, and bury'd him in it with *Duhaut*, doing them more Honour than they had done to Monfieur *de la Sale* and his Nephew *Moranget*, whom they left to be devour'd by wild Beafts. Thus thofe Murderers met with what they had deferv'd, dying the fame Death they had put others to.

The Natives, *Hiens* had brought with him, having been Spectators of that Murder, were in a Confternation, and that Affair was of dangerous Confequence to us, who ftood in Need of them. It was therefore requifite to make the beft of it, giving them to underftand, that there had been Reafon for fo punifhing thofe dead Perfons, becaufe they had all the Powder and Ball, and would not give any to the reft. They remain'd fatisfy'd with that Excufe, and he who was call'd *Larcheveque*, and who was entirely devoted to *Duhaut*, being Abroad a hunting fince the Morning, and not knowing what Misfortune

tune

May 1687.

tune had hapned his Protector, and *Hiens* being resolv'd to make away with him, Father *Anastasius* and Monsieur *Cavelier* took so much Pains, that they dissuaded him from it, and I went out and met *Larcheveque*, to give him Notice of that Disaster, and to inform him, how he was to behave himself. Thus I requited him for having come to give me Notice of Monsieur *de la Sale*'s Death. I brought him to *Hiens*, who declar'd he design'd him no Harm, and *Larcheveque* gave him the same Assurances on his Part. Thus all Things are again compos'd, and nothing remain'd, but for us to set out, but first to know what we were to do, and which Way to direct our Course.

Hereupon, *Heins* took upon him to speak, and said, he had promis'd the Natives to go to the War with them, and design'd to be as good as his Word; that if we would expect his Return, we might by that Time consider which Way he would move, and that in the mean Time we might stay in the Village among the *Cenis*. This was resolv'd on; we loaded all our Effects on our Horses, and repair'd to the same Place and the same Cottage, where we had been before, the Chief of it assigning us the one Half to lodge and lay up our Baggage.

When the Day for setting out for the War was come, *Hiens* departed with the Natives, four of our Comrades and the two half Savage *French* Men going along with him; so that there were six of them, and each took a Horse. *Hiens* left us all the Effects, and desir'd we would stay for him, which we promis'd, not knowing how to avoid it, considering, that the *Indians* might have

Six French Men go to the Wars with the Natives.

May 1687 have done us Harm, and even have obſtructed our Departure. Thus we reſign'd ourſelves to Providence, and remain'd ſix of us together, *viz.* Father *Anaſtaſius,* Monſieur *Cavalier,* his Nephew young *Cavelier,* young *Talon,* another Youth of *Paris,* and I. There alſo remain'd ſome old Men, who could not go to the War, and the Women. We were alſo join'd by two other *French* Men, who had been left on the other Side the River, being the *Provencal* and one *Teiſſier.*

Bewailing the Memory of Men kill'd.
During our Stay, and our Warriors being abroad upon that Expedition, the old Men often viſited us, and told us News from the Army by Signs, which we underſtood nothing of. We were from Time to Time alarm'd, ſeeing the Women weep, without any viſible Cauſe. The late Monſieur *de la Sale* had often told us, that the Women bewail'd thoſe that were to be kill'd; but we were inform'd, that they did ſo, when they call'd to Mind ſome who had been ſlain in the former Wars; which diſpell'd our Apprehenſions. However we were uneaſy, becauſe thoſe old Men and Women examin'd us every Morning and Evening when we perform'd our Devotions.

We laid hold of that Opportunity to give them to underſtand, that we paid our Duty to one God, the only Supreme Sovereign of all Things, pointing to Heaven, and endeavouring in the beſt Manner we were able, to ſignify to them that he was Almighty, that he had made all Things, that he caus'd the Earth to produce it's Fruits to proſper, and the Growth of it, which maintain'd them to thrive; but this being only by Signs, they did not underſtand us, and we labour'd in vain.

The

Some Time after, Monfieur *Moranget* re-turn'd, gave Monfieur *de la Sale* an Account of his fhort Journey, and faid, That one of the Natives, vvho favv us the Night before, came to meet and conduct him to the Chief's Cottage, where forty ancient *Indians* were, by vvhom he had been kindly receiv'd. That the Chief had in his Hand a Reed, at the End whereof was made faft a Leaf of a *French* Book, which he had an extraordinary Refpect for. That they had been made to fit on Bullocks Hides, and treated with dry'd Beef.

That after thefe firft Ceremonies, the Chief had given them to underftand, that fome of their People had been conducted by a Man like us, to our Habitation, and that the faid Man had promis'd to bring them to talk with us, in order to treat of Peace ; but that on the Contrary, we had fired on them and kill'd one of their Men, which had oblig'd them to kill the Man that led them, and that then they return'd. It is not improper here to put the Reader in Mind, that I have before mention'd this Accident, when the Sieur *Barbier* croffing the River in a Canoe, was call'd upon by fome Perfon, who was among the Natives on the Bank of the River, vvho had made two Shots, as it had been only the Priming of a Piece, vvhich the Sieur *Barbier* had look'd upon as an Infult, and therefore he had alfo fir'd, vvith all the other Particulars, as mention'd before ; an Accident that happen'd for vvant of underftanding one another ; vvhich, together with Monfr. *de la Sale*'s forbidding us to have any Communication with the Natives, vvas very prejudicial to us afterwards.

After

After much other Diſcourſe, Monſieur *Mo-ranget* having given them ſome ſmall Preſents, they made their Return in Bullocks Hides, and Goats Skins well dreſs'd. He ask'd them for ſome Horſes to barter; they anſwer'd, they had no more than what they ſtood in Need of. We immediately proceeded on our Journey, and that Day being the 21ſt, went to incamp at the Edge of a Wood.

The 22d, we went up to an Eminence ter-minated by a Rock, at the Foot whereof ran a little River, the Bottom whereof was all of flat Rocks, fit for Building. Thence we deſcry'd two Natives driving of Bullocks, which made us ſtand upon our Guard, and it appear'd to be our *Indian*, who had met another, with whom he had been acquainted among the *Cenis*, and whom he had brought along with him.

Three loſt French Men heard of.

Monſieur *de la Sale* was very glad to ſee him, and remember'd he was one of thoſe of whom he had purchas'd a Horſe. He ask'd ſeveral Queſtions of him, and among the reſt, whether he had not ſeen the four Men who deſerted in his former Journey, or heard any Talk of the others, to whom he had given Leave to return to our Dwelling. He anſwer'd, he had ſeen one among the *Cenis*, and two others among the *Aſſonis*; but that he had not heard of any more, and that they muſt needs be dead; as alſo the Sieur *Bihorel*, who was likewiſe men-tion'd to him.

He further told us, that there were four or five Cottages thereabouts, in which about Fif-teen Men reſided. At Night he went away. Our *Indian* had kill'd a Cow at a great Diſtance and ſhot her quite through, at which the other,
vvho

who had been an Eye Witneſs to it, ſtood a *Feb.* 1687
long Time amaz'd, without ſpeaking one
Word, admiring the Effect of our Pieces. That
Cow was ſent for, and the Fleſh brought to
our Camp.

The 23d, we paſs'd by the Cottages we had
been told of, where the Natives were with
their Wives and Children. Monſr. *de la Sale*
caus'd us to halt in the Village. We were well
receiv'd, they preſented us with dry'd Beef, and
we return'd it in ſome Knives. We ſaw two
Horſes, one of them a little grey, indifferent
handſome. They told us they would ſoon depart that Place, to go join their Companions,
who were in War with their Enemies. The reſt
of our Men being come up, we went on to
incamp a League from thence, on the Bank of a
Rivulet, and at the Foot of one of the higheſt
Mountains in the Country.

Unloading our Horſes, we perceiv'd there
wanted a large Axe, which ſerv'd us for hewing down of Trees. Monſieur *de la Sale* ſent
his *Indian* to demand it, at the Village we came
from laſt, the Savages ſaid they had not ſeen
it, and it was loſt. He brought back Word,
that the Savages had told him, that if we would
ſtay for them, they would go along with, and
ſhew us the Way.

However, we went on the 24th, and incamp'd on the Edge of a Marſh. The 25th,
the Rain hinder'd us from Marching. The
26th, Monſieur *de la Sale* perceiving how difficult and dangerous it was to croſs that Marſh,
ſent his *Indian* to the others, to know whether
they really deſign'd to go with us. They anſwer'd, we muſt return thither to join them.
                                                    The

Mar. 1687 The 27th. we decamp'd, in order to it; but took another Way to go meet the *Indians*. The 28th. we faw them marching at a Diftance. One of them was detach'd to come tell us, that he would fhew us the Way to crofs the Marfh, and we went on and incamp'd at the Foot of the high Mountain I have fpoken of.

The firft of *March*, we join'd the *Indians*, on the Edge of the Marfh, which we had juft crofs'd, where the Rains kept us till the Fifth, during which Time we went to find out where we might pafs a rapid Torrent, that difcharges it felf into the River call'd of *Canoes*, which we pafs'd the 6th, in the Canoe we had made, and which did us good Service, to pafs other Rivers we met with the 7th and the 8th on our Way.

The 9th, we did not ftir, becaufe of the Rain. *River of Canoes.* The 10th, incamp'd on the Bank of a fmall River, which we crofs'd the 11th, and the fame Day another River, and incamp'd on the Bank of it, and found it adorn'd with very fine Mulberry Trees. The 12th we crofs'd another River, and incamp'd near it. The 13th, came again to the River of *Canoes*, fo call'd by Monfieur *de la Sale*, becaufe he the firft Time put Canoes into it, at his former Journey. We pafs'd it the 14th, and incamped on the other Side where we again join'd the *Indians*.

The 15th, we held on our Journey with them and found a pleafanter Country than that we had pafs'd thro'; and Monfieur *de la Sale* having in his former Journey hid fome Indian Wheat *Provifions hid, fpoilt.* and Beans, two or three Leagues from that Place, and our Provifions beginning to fall fhort, it was thought fit to go to that Place. Accordingly he order'd the Sieurs *Duhaut*, *Hiens*, *Lio-*

tot

tot the Surgeon, his own *Indian*, and his Footman, whose Name was *Saget*, who were follow-
ed by some Natives, to go to the Place he described to them, where they found all rotten
and quite spoilt.

The 16, in their Return, they met with two
Bullocks, which Monsieur *de la Sale*'s *Indian*
kill'd, whereupon they sent back his Footman,
to give him Notice of what they had kill'd, that
if he would have the Flesh dry'd, he might
send Horses for it. The 17th, Monsieur *de la
Sale* had the Horses taken up, and order'd the
Sieurs *Moranget* and *de Male* and his Footman,
to go for that Meat, and send back a Horse
Load immediately, till the rest was dry'd.

Monsieur *Moranget*, when he came thither,
found they had smoak'd both the Beeves, tho' *occasion'd*
they were not dry enough; and the said Sieurs *by Monsr.*
Liotot, *Hiens*, *Duhaut* and the rest had laid aside Moran-
the Marrow-Bones and others to roast them, *get.*
and eat the Flesh that remain'd on them, as was
usual to do. The Sieur *Moranget* found fault
with it, he in a Passion seiz'd not only the Flesh
that was smoak'd and dry'd, but also the Bones,
without giving them any Thing; but on the
contrary, threatning they should not eat so much
of it, as they had imagin'd, and that he would
manage that Flesh after another Manner.

This passionate Behaviour, so much out of
Season, and contrary to Reason and Custom, *to murder*
touch'd the Surgeon *Liotot*, *Heins* and *Duhaut* *Monsr.* de
to the Quick, they having other Causes of Com- *la Sale.*
plaint against *Moranget*. They withdrew, and
resolv'd together upon a bloody Revenge; they
agreed upon the Manner of it, and concluded
they would murder the Sieur *Moranget*, Mon-

H   sieur

fieur *de la Sale*'s Footman and his *Indian*, becaufe he was very faithful to him.

They waited till Night, when thofe unfortunate Creatures had fupp'd and were afleep. *Liotot* the Surgeon was the inhuman Executioner, he took an Ax, began by the Sieur *Moranget*, giving him many Strokes on the Head; the

Bloody Murderers fame he did by the Footman and the *Indian*, killing them on the Spot, whilft his Fellow Villains, *viz.* *Duhaut*, *Hiens*, *Teiffier* and *Larcheveque* ftood upon their Guard, with their Arms, to fire upon fuch as fhould make any Refiftance. The *Indian* and the Footman never ftir'd, but the Sieur *Moranget* had fo much Vigour as to fit up, but without being able to fpeak one Word, and the Affafins obliged the Sieur *de Marle* to make an End of him, tho' he was not in the Confpiracy.

This Slaughter had yet fatisfy'd but one Part of the Revenge of thofe Murderers. To finifh

Confult to murder Monfr. de la Sale. it and fecure themfelves it was requifite to deftroy the Commander in Chief. They confulted about the fafeft Method to effect it, and refolve to go together to Monfieur *de la Sale*, to knock out the Brains of the moft refolute immediately, and then it would be eafier to overcome the reft. But the River, which was between them and us, being much fwollen, the Difficulty of paffing it made them put it off the 18th and 19th. On the other Hand Monfieur *de la Sale* was very uneafy, on Account of their long Stay. His Impatience made him refolve to go himfelf to find out his People and to know the Caufe of it.

This was not done without many previous Tokens of Concern, and Apprehenfion. He

seem'd

seem'd to have some Presage of his Misfortune, enquiring of some, whether the Sieur *Liotot*, *Hiens* and *Duhaut* had not express'd some Discontent ; and not hearing any Thing of it, he could not forbear setting out the 20th, with Father *Anastasius* and an *Indian*, leaving me the Command in his Absence, and charging me from Time to Time to go the Rounds about our Camp, to prevent being surpriz'd, and to make a Smoke for him to direct his Way in Case of Need. When he came near the Dwelling of the Murderers, looking out sharp to discover something, he observed Eagles fluttering about a Spot, not far from them, which made him believe they had found some Carrion about the Mansion, and he fired a Shot, which was the Signal of his Death and forwarded it.

The Conspirators hearing the Shot, concluded it was Monsieur *de la Sale*, who was come to seek them. They made ready their Arms and provided to surprize him. *Duhaut* passed the River, with *Larcheveque*. The first of them spying Monsieur *de la Sale* at a Distance, as he was coming towards them, advanc'd and hid himself among the high Weeds, to wait his passing by, so that Monsieur *de la Sale* suspecting nothing, and having not so much as charg'd his Piece again, saw the aforesaid *Larcheveque* at a good Distance from him, and immediately ask'd for his Nephew *Moranget*, to which *Larcheveque* answer'd, That he was along the River. At the same Time the Traitor *Duhaut* fired his Piece and shot Monsr. *de la Sale* thro' the Head, so that he dropp'd down dead on the Spot, without speaking one Word.

Father *Anaftafius*, who was then by his Side,
ftood ftock ftill in a Fright, expecting the fame
Fate, and not knowing whether he fhould go
forwards or backwards ; but the Murderer
Duhaut put him out of that Dread, bidding him
not to fear, for no Hurt was intended him ;
that it was Defpair that had prevail'd with him
to do what he faw ; that he had long defired
to be revenged on *Moranget*, becaufe he had
defign'd to ruin him, and that he was partly
the Occafion of his Uncle's Death. This is the
exact Relation of that Murder, as it was prefently after told me by F. *Anaftafius*.

Such was the unfortunate End of Monfieur
de la Sale's·Life, at a Time when he might en-
His Cha-
racter.
tertain the greateft Hopes, as the Reward of
his Labours. He had a Capacity and Talent
to make his Enterprize fuccefsful ; his Conftancy
and Courage and his extraordinary Knowledge
in Arts and Sciences, which render'd him fit
for any Thing, together with an indefatigable
Body, which made him furmount all Difficulties,
would have procur'd a glorious Iffue to his Undertaking, had not all thofe excellent Qualities
been counterbalanced by too haughty a Behaviour, which fometimes made him infupporta-
ble, and by a Rigidnefs towards thofe that
were under his Command, which at laft drew
on him an implacable Hatred, and was the Occafion of his Death.

The Shot which had kill'd Monfieur *de la Sale*,
was alfo a Signal of the Murder to the Affaffins
for them to draw near. They all repair'd to
the Place where the wretched dead Corps lay,
Barbarity
towards
the dead
Body.
which they barbaroufly ftrip'd to the Shirt, and
vented their Malice in vile and opprobrious
Language.

Language. The Surgeon *Liotot* said several Times in Scorn and Derision, *There thou liest, Great Bassa, there thou liest.* In Conclusion, they dragged it naked among the Bushes, and left it exposed to the ravenous Wild Beasts. So far was it from vvhat a certain Author writes, of their having bury'd him and set up a Cross on his Grave.

When those Murderers had satiated their Rage, they set out to come to us at our Camp, with the dry'd Flesh, which they had caus'd to be brought over the River by the *Indians*, who had been Spectators of the Murder and of all the inhuman Actions that had been committed, with Amazement and Contempt of us. When they were come to the Camp, they found Messieurs *Cavelier*, the one Brother, the other Nephew to the murder'd Commander, whom Father *Anastasius* acquainted with the dismal End of our Chief, and enjoyn'd them Silence, which it is easy to imagine was very hard upon them; but it was absolutely necessary.

However, Monsieur *Cavelier* the Priest, could not forbear telling them, that if they would do the same by him, he would forgive them his Murder, and only desir'd them to give him a Quarter of an Hour to prepare himself: They answer'd, They had Nothing to say to him; that what they had done was the Effect of Despair, to be reveng'd for the ill Usage they had receiv'd.

I was absent at that Time; he they call'd *Larcheveque*, who, as I have said, was one of the Conspirators, had some Kindness for me, and knowing they design'd to make me away too, if

Mar.1687

Murderers return to the Camp.

H. 3   I stood

Mar. 1687 I stood upon my Defence, he parted from them, to give me Notice of their mischievous Resolution. He found me on a little rising Ground, where I was looking upon our Horses as they graz'd in a little adjacent Bottom. His Intelligence struck me to the Heart, not knowing *The Author* whether I should fly or stay; but at length, ha-*sav'd by a* ving neither Powder nor Shot, nor Arms, and *Friend.* the said *Larcheveque* giving me Assurances of my Life, provided I was quiet and said Nothing, I committed my self to God's Protection, and went to them, without taking any Notice of what had been done.

Dehaut, *Dehaut,* puff'd up with his new gotten Autho-*the Mur-* rity, procur'd him by his Villany, as soon as he *derer, u-* saw me, cry'd out, Every Man ought to com-*jurps the* mand in his Turn; to which I made no An-*Command.* swer; and we were all of us oblig'd to stifle our Resentment, that it might not appear, for our Lives depended on it. However, it was easy to judge with what Eyes Father *Anastasius,* Messieurs *Cavelier* and I beheld these Murderers, to whom we expected every Moment to fall Sacrifices. It is true, we dissembled so well, that they were not very suspicious of us, and that the Temptation we were under of making them away in Revenge for those they had murder'd, would have easily prevail'd and been put in Execution, had not Monsieur *Cavelier,* the Priest, always positively oppos'd it, alledging, that we ought to leave Vengeance to God.

March However the Murderers seiz'd upon all the *continued.* Effects, without any Opposition, and then we began to talk of proceeding on our Journey.

We

We decamp'd the 21st, with our *Indians*, and march'd with such a heavy Rain, that we were oblig'd to halt on the Bank of a great Stream, where one of theNatives that had left us, arriv'd with his Wife. We went on the 22d and 23d, and pass'd the River, where Father *Anastasius*, Monsieur *Cavelier* and I, who could not swim, had been drown'n, but that the Natives assisted and sav'd us. The 24th, we went on thro' a marshy Country, never quitting a small Path which led to the Village of the *Cenis*, till the 28th, when we rested on the Bank of a River *Cenis Ri-* of the same Name, tho' about ten Leagues di- *ver.* stant from the Village.

We had hop'd to ford that River, as Monsieur *de la Sale* had done, when he return'd from that Country; but it was so swollen, that there was no doing it, and we were forced to make a Canoe of Bullocks Hides. Whilst we were employ'd at that Work, the *Indians* swam over and went to give Notice to the *Cenis* of our Arrival.

We found the Country pleasant enough about that River, tho' the Land did not seem to be any of the best; but still it was delightful to the Eye, well planted with fine Trees of seve-ral Sorts, among which, is one that Monsieur *de la Sale* had nam'd *Copal*, being very beautiful, *Copal* the Leaves of it between those of the Maple *Tree.* and the Lime Trees in Resemblance, and from it comes a Gum, of a very agreeable Scent. In the same Place we saw a great Tree, on which the late Monsieur *de la Sale* had caus'd Crosses and the Arms of *France* to be carv'd.

The

The Hunting of Bullocks had fail'd us, and we had seen none from the Place where our late Leader had been murder'd. Thus our Provisions began to fall short, and it was resolv'd on the 29th, to send some Men before, to the Village of the *Cenis*, to know, whether they had any *Indian* Corn, and were willing to barter for it. I was appointed, with the Surgeon *Liotot*, the *Tessieers*, and *Hiens*, vvho was a Buccanier, Monsieur *de la Sale* had taken up at *Petit Gouave*, to go with him upon this Expedition. I was very unwilling to undertake that Journey, with a Murderer and two of his Companions, of whom I was suspicious; but it was very requisite to obey, and *Duhaut* having all the Effects in his Possession, alledging, that a great Part of them belong'd to him, he gave us some Axes and Knives to barter for *Indian* Corn, as also for Horses, if any were to be had, and accordingly we pass'd the River.

The Author sent to the Cenis for Provisions.

The Country describ'd.

We found the Country made up of several little Hills, of an indifferent Height, on which there are Abundance of Wallnut-Trees and Oaks, not so large as what we had seen before, but very agreeable. The Weeds which had been some Time before burnt by the Natives, began to spring up again, and discover'd large green Fields very pleasing to the Sight.

When we had travell'd some Time, we discover'd three Men a Horseback, coming towards us from the Village, and being come near them, saw one dress'd after the *Spanish* Fashion, with a little Doublet, the Body wherof was of blue, and the Sleeves of white Fustian,

Fuſtian, as it were imbroider'd, with very
ſtreight Breeches, white worſted Stockings,
Woollen-Garters, a broad-brim'd, flat-crown'd
Hat, and long Hair. We preſently concluded
he was a *Spaniard*, and the rather becauſe we
had been told, that ſome of them were to come
to join in League with the *Cenis*, againſt an E-
nemy Nation, and we were at a Nonplus ; for
if vve fell into their Hands, we muſt never expect to get away, but be condemn'd to ſerve
either in the Mines, or in the Quarries, in the
Kingdom of *Mexico*, for which Reaſon we provided to give the pretended *Spaniard* an unkind
Reception, and then to make the beſt of our
Way back.

Mar. 1687

*A Man
clad like a
Spaniard.*

Being come up to him, I ſpoke ſome Words
of *Spaniſh* and *Italian*, to which he return'd
no Anſwer ; but on the contrary, made uſe
of the Word *Couſſica*, which in the Language of the *Cenis*, ſignifies, *I do not underſtand you* ; which Anſwer of his remov'd our
Apprehenſions. The two others were quite
naked, one of them being mounted on a
fine grey Mare, and on her were beſides
two Panniers, handſomly made of Reeds, full
of very fine Meal parch'd, or roaſted. After ſeveral Queſtions, to which we had no
very ſatisfactory Anſwers, we lighted Fire to
make them ſmoke, and then they preſented
us with the two Panniers full of Meal, giving us to underſtand, that their Chief expected us in the Village, and having ſignify'd, that they were ſent to meet us, we
gave them ſome Knives and Strings of
Beads.

We

Mar. 1687
We ask'd them, whether they had any Men among them like him that was a Horseback in the *Spanish* Habit, they anfwer'd, there were two in a Neighbouring Nation, call'd *Affony*, and that he who was clad, had been in their Country, and brought thence the Cloaths we faw him wear. That Man then fhew'd us a *Spanish* printed Paper, containing the Indulgences granted to the Miffioners of *New Mexico*. After this they left us to go on, to our People, for which Reafon I writ a Note, giving an Account of our having met them.

We alighted to eat, and let our Horfes graze on the Bank of a Rivulet; but it was not long before the fame Natives, who had been with us before, appear'd again hard by us. We made Signs to them to draw near and eat with us; which they did, and then went along with us towards the Village, which we would not go into, becaufe it was Night. The *Indian* that was clad, ftay'd all Night with us, and the two others went away.

When it was Day, we held on our Way to the Village; the *Indian* that was with us con-*The Cenis meet the French in folemn Manner.* ducting us to their Chief's Cottage. By the Way, we faw many other Cottages, and the Elders coming to meet us in their Formalities, which confifted in fome GoatsSkins drefs'd and painted of feveral Colours, which they wore on their Shoulders like Belts, and Plumes of Feathers of feveral Colours, on their Heads, like Coronets. Six or feven of them had fquare Sword Blades, like the *Spanish*, on the Hilts whereof they had faften'd great Plumes of Feathers, and feveral Hawks Bells; fome of them had Clubs, which they call Head-breakers, fome
only

only their Bows and Arrows; others, Bits of
white Linen, reaching from Shoulder to Shoulder. All their Faces were daub'd vvith black
or red. There were twelve Elders, who walk'd
in the Middle, and the Youth and Warriors in
Ranks, on the Sides of those old Men.

Being come up to us in that Manner, he
that conducted us, made a Sign for us to halt,
vvhich vvhen vve had done, all the old Men
lifted up their Right Hands above their Heads,
crying out in a moſt ridiculous Manner; but
it behov'd us to have a Care of laughing. That
done, they came and imbrac'd us, uſing all Sorts
of Endearments. Then they made us ſmoke, *A French*
and brought to us a French Man of *Provence*, *Man a-*
vvho vvas one of thoſe that had forſaken the *mong the*
late Monſieur *de la Sale*, at his firſt Journey. *Indians.*

The vvhole Company conducted us after the
ſame Manner, to their Chief's Cottage; and after we had ſtaid there a ſhort Time, they led us
to a larger Cottage, a Quarter of a League
from thence, being the Hut in vvhich they have
their publick Rejoycings, and the great Aſſemblies. We found it furniſh'd with Mats for *Indian En-*
us to ſit on. The Elders ſeated themſelves round *tertain-*
about us, and they brought us to eat, ſome *ment.*
Sagamite, which is their Pottage, little Beans,
Bread made of *Indian* Corn, and another Sort
they make vvith boil'd Flower, and at laſt they
made us ſmoke.

. During our Repaſt, they entertain'd us vvith
the Diſcouſe of their Deſign to make War on
a Nation, vvho vvere their Enemies, and whom
they call'd *Cannokantimo*. When it vvas over,
vve preſented them, according to Cuſtom,
vvith ſome Knives and Strings of Beads for
their

their Wives. We defir'd them to afford us fome *Indian* Corn, in Exchange for other Things, vvhich they promis'd, and the French Man vvho vvas vvith them, having told us, that there vvas a Diftrict, vvhich afforded more Corn, than that vvhere vve vvere, and vvhere his Cottage vvas, vve refolv'd to go thither. We propos'd it to the Elders, vvho would needs go along vvith us, attended by a great Number of Youth, and having got ready our Horfes, vve fet out for that Place.

By the Way, we faw feveral Cottages at certain Diftances, ftragling up and down, as the Ground happens to te fit for Tillage. The Field lies about the Cottage, and at other Di-ftances there are other large Huts, not inha-bited, but only ferving for publick Affemblies, either upon Occafion of Rejoycings, or to con-fult about Peace and War.

Huts and Families in them. The Cottages that are inhabited, are not each of them for a private Family, for in fome of them there are fifteen or twenty, each of which has its Nook or Corner, Bed and other Utenfils to its felf; but without any Partition to feparate it from the reft: However, they have Nothing in Common befides the Fire, which is in the Midft of the Hut, and never goes out. It is made of great Trees, the Ends whereof are laid together, fo that when once lighted, it lafts a long Time, and the firft Comer takes Care to keep it up.

Manner of Building. The Cottages are round at the Top, after the Manner of a Bee-Hive, or a Reek of Hay. Some of them are fixty Foot Diameter. In Or-der to build them, they plant Trees as thick as a Man's Thigh, tall and ftrait, and placing
them

We kill'd five Beeves at the Entrance into the Wood, forded the River, and incamp'd Half a League beyond it, whence Monſieur *de la Sale* ſent Men vvith the Horſes, to bring the Fleſh of the Bullocks vve had kill'd ; the Hides of them, which ſerv'd to cover us, being very uſeful againſt a violent Shower of Rain that fell.

The 14th, the Rain ceaſing, we travell'd over another ſpacious Plain, vvhere there is a Multitude of Beeves and Wild Fowl. We ſaw ſeveral Tracks, leading every Way, made by the Bullocks, of which we ſaw ſeveral Herds, ſome moving on haſtily, and others running out-right, which made us ſuppoſe they were drove by the Natives. In ſhort, having halted to help up one of our Horſes that was fallen, we ſaw an *Indian* following them very cloſe. Monſieur *de la Sale* caus'd a Horſe to be immediately unloaded, which a Man mounting, rode after, overtook and brought the *Indian*.

When the Savage ſaw himſelf among us, he concluded he was a loſt Man, he quak'd for Fear, and not without Reaſon, for moſt of our Men had reſov'd to kill him ; Monſieur *de la Sale* oppos'd it, alledging, that vve vvere but a ſmall Number, that very few were left behind at the Habitation, and therefore vve ought not to render our ſelves odious to the Natives, but to uſe them kindly, that we might have Peace ; an infallible Maxim, the Practice of which might have been fortunate to him, had he follow'd it ſooner.

He

He therefore caus'd a Fire to be made, gave him to Eat and Smoke, and afterwards a Bit of Roll-Tabacco, and ſome other Trifles: Monſieur *de la Sale* gave him to underſtand, that he came not to hurt any Man, but to ſettle Peace in all Places, and ſo diſmiſs'd him. The *Indian* recover'd himſelf a little of his Fright; but being ſtill dubious, what his Fate might be, he at firſt walk'd away gently, ſtill looking about him, and when at a good Diſtance, made off as faſt as he could. We held on our Way, and ſoon after ſaw another *Indian* running after the Bullocks. Monſieur *de la Sale* caus'd him to be taken, brought to us, and treated as the firſt had been.

We had not gone far before we ſpy'd a Company of Natives coming towards us, on our left, but we held on our Way, till they were over againſt us,, when Monſieur *de la Sale* caus'd us to halt. The Savages ſeeing us halt, ſtood ſtill alſo, which Monſieur *de la Sale* perceiving, he laid his Firelock on the Ground, and advanc'd towards them, making Signs to him that Commanded them, who was a handſome Man, to draw near. That *Indian* came forward, and was follow'd by the reſt, all of them Careſſing us after their Manner, which we return'd the beſt we were able, and then made them Smoak.

Natives entertain'd

Next Monſieur *de la Sale* gave them to underſtand, that we were going towards the *Cenis,* that we deſir'd to be at Peace with them all, and that we would return to our own Country, whence we would bring them all they had Occaſion for. Then we diſtributed among them ſome Bits of Roll-Tabacco, ſome Strings of Beads

Beads and Knives, which they feem'd to be *Jan.* 1687
pleas'd with, and all this was done by Signs.
Then every Man went his own Way :
We advanc'd half a League farther, to get into
a Wood, where Monfieur *de la Sale* had encamp'd when he went that Way before ; we
cut down Trees to fecure our Poft, and lay
there that Night.

Before our Intrenchment was finifh'd, we difcover'd, firft one *Indian*, then two, and afterwards three, coming one after another ; which
giving Monfieur *de la Sale* fome Jealoufy, he
caus'd us to handle our Arms, with Orders to
ftand upon our Guard, for fear of being furpriz'd, and went towards them. They fignify'd to him, that their People had told them,
we did not hurt any Body, which was very well,
and that they were come to fee us. They were
entertain'd as the others had been, and then
Signs were made them to withdraw, becaufe
Night drew on, and having obferv'd, that they
took Notice of our fortifying our felves, vve
kept a good Guard all the Night, vvithout any
Difturbance.

The Fifteenth, vve march'd on, intending to
find out a Ford, in the River call'd of the *Princefs*,
vvhere Monfieur *de la Sale* had pafs'd before ;
but miffing of it, and the River being fwollen,
vve vvere oblig'd to go up higher, fometimes
croffing curious Meadows, and fometimes
Woods of tall Trees of feveral Sorts, but all *A fine*
Young of the fame Thicknefs and ftrait, look- *Country.*
ing as if they had been planted by a Line. The
River running through the midft of thofe curious fhady Groves, which were alfo water'd by

G   feveral

Jan.1687 ſeveral little Brooks of very clear and good Water, afforded a moſt delightful Landskip.

Thick Woods. We alſo met with ſome Woods ſo thick, that that it was requiſite to hew a Paſſage for the Horſes. Towards the Evening we kill'd a Bullock, and went to incamp in a little Coppice, with our uſual Precautions.

WildFowl. The 16th, we continued our Journey, ſtill following the River upwards, and from Time to Time meeting the ſame Sort of Paſture Grounds and the Obſtacles of Woods, where we were fain to cut our Way through, which fatigued us very much ; but the Plenty of wild Fowl, and particularly of Turkeys, whereof we killed many, was an Eaſe to our Sufferings, and Help to bear our Toil with more Satiſfaction.

An Indian Village a-bandon'd. The 17th, was a very toilſome Day's Journey, by Reaſon of the Woods and Rivulets we were to croſs ; after which we came to a little Hill, on which there were 2 or 300 Cottages of the Natives. Thoſe Huts were like large Ovens, conſiſting of long Poles ſtuck in the Earth in a Circle, and joyning above to make the Dome or round Top. They had been a Dwelling of the Natives, who being gone, had carry'd away the Hides that cover'd them, and the Mats which are us'd to hang the Inſides, and to make their Beds of.

After a March of ſome Hours, our *Indian* having found a Herd of Beeves, we kill'd ſeven or eight, took the beſt of the Meat, and held on our Way acroſs a Wood. We forded a Branch of the River, and proceeded to the Bank of another, the the Bottom whereof being foul, we incamp'd on the Edge of it, and the Rain falling

at

at Night and continuing all the next Day, were
oblig'd to stay there.

The 19th, the Rain ceasing, we proceeded
through a thick Fog, and over Places where
the Water was often up to our Knees, and
sometimes higher; vvhich, together with our
being forc'd to cut the Way athwart the Bushes,
vvith our Hatchets, gave us inexpressible Trouble, and it had been much greater, had vve not
resolv'd to follovv the Ways beaten by the
Bullocks, vvhom a natural Instinct alvvays leads
to those Parts vvhich are easiest to pass.

We were not free from another Inconveniency in those Tracks, which was their being
full of Water and very rugged, a Thing no
Way agreeable to our Shoes, which were no
other than a Piece of Bullocks Hide or Goats
Skin quite green, whereof we made a Sort of
Buskins, to serve instead of Shoes, but when
those wretched Boots were dry'd by the Heat,
upon our Feet, they hurt us very much, and
we were often oblig'd to set our Feet in the
the Water, to soften those Buskins. However,
we march'd all the Day, notwithstanding all
those Inconveniences, without finding a proper
Place to incamp, and at last came to a River,
whose high Bank afforded us a Spot to rest on.

Buskins of raw Hides instead of Shoes.

The 20th, a small Rain did not obstruct our
March, and having cross'd a Wood, half a
League athwart, and a Marsh of the same Extent, we came into a large Plain, cut across by
great Tracks of Bullocks, which went towards
the River, and made us suppose there might
be a Ford. We follow'd that Way, but found
the River so swollen, and its Stream so rapid,
that it was impossible to cross it, but were o-

blig'd

*Jan.*1687 blig'd to halt upon its Bank, whence we went to hunt Bullocks, whereof we had no Want, nor of Turkeys and other wild Fowl.

The 21th, we proceeded up that River, and found a narrow deep Place, near which we hew'd down a Tree, making it fall ſo as to reach from the one Bank to the other, in the Nature of a Plank, and handed our Baggage from one to another over it. The Horſes ſwam over and we incamp'd on the other Side, near a very beautiful Plain.

Hebaha-mo, *Indian Nation.*

Whilſt we were hewing down ſome little Wood to intrench ourſelves, we heard a Voice, whereupon handling our Arms and going to the Place where we heard it, we ſaw a Company of fifteen Savages, who were coming towards us, and made Signs to us to go to them, laying down their Bows, in Token of Peace. We alſo made our Sign to them to draw near, they did ſo and careſs'd us after their Manner. We made them ſit down and ſmoke, after which, Monſr. *de la Sale* began to converſe with them by Signs, and by Help of ſome Words of the Language of the *Cenis*, which he was skilful in, he underſtood, that theſe vvere their Neighbours and Allies; that their Village was not far off, and that their Nation was call'd *Hebahamo*. Some ſmall Preſents were given them and they vvithdrew, promiſing to return the next Day.

The 22th, our Horſes being ſpent and hurt, and we much tir'd, the Day was given to Reſt, and the Natives did not fail to come, being twenty five in Number, ſome of whom had Bucklers or Targets made of the ſtrongſt Part of the Bullocks Hides. They gave us to underſtand, that they were ingag'd in War towards the *N W.*

and

and told us, they had seen Men like us, vvho vvere but ten Days Journey from that Place. Other Tokens they gave, made us suppose it was *New Spain* that they talk'd of.

Monsr. *de la Sale* took several Words of their Language, vvhich is very different from that of the *Cenis*, and more difficult. As for their Customs, they are much alike. Infine, having shewn us, that towards the *N.W.* we should meet with Plains, vvhere the Way would be easier, and we should shun the Woods, we gave them to eat, and some Presents, and they took Leave of us. A Rain falling and holding all the Night, we did not march the 24th. The 25th, we travell'd not far, by Reason of the Rains continuing, and that there were several Rivers in the Way much swollen.

The 16th, we proceeded on our Journey, and came to the River call'd *la Sabloniere*, from the many Sand Banks there are in it. The 27th, departing from it, we came to another little narrow River, but very deep ; going up higher we found a Ford, and went to incamp beyond it, in a little Wood, where we had a very bad Night, because of the Rain which fell again, and the o- verflowing of the River, which oblig'd us to make a little Sort of Scaffold, to lay our Powder and Cloaths on, that they might not be wet. The next Day being the 28th, observing that the Water was still rising, we decamp'd to go a League farther, to a higher Ground, where we made a great Fire to warm and dry us.

We took Notice the Country was very good, the Plains extending as far as the Eye could reach, and adorn'd with many little Coppices, affording a very agreeable Prospect. We march'd over Part of them the 29th and 30th, after 3 Hours

Travel, found a Way full of Water, which oblig'd
us to incamp on the Bank of a River; pass'd it the
31th, and incamp'd in a Wood close by.

Village in-
habited.
The next Day, being the First of *February*
1687, Monsieur *de la Sale* left me to guard the
Camp, and took along with him, Monsieur *Ca-*
velier his Brother and seven Men, to go see
whether he could find any Body in several Cottages our Hunters had discover'd. He found
twenty four or twenty five of them, built round
like those I have before mention'd, standing
on a rising Ground, almost encompass'd by the
River, in each of which there were four or five
Men, and several Women and Children.

The Savages were somewhat surpriz'd at
Monsieur *de la Sale*'s coming; however they
receiv'd him in friendly Manner, and conducted him to their Commander's Hut, which was
immediately fill'd with People, who came to see
him. The Elders came together there, Bullocks Hides were laid upon the Ground, on
which they made Monsieur *de la Sale* and his
Company sit. They gave them hung Beef to
eat, and then signify'd to them that some
of their 'Allies had given them Notice of
our being in the Country, and that we were
going to the *Cenis*, and they had imagin'd that
we would pass thro' their Country.

Monsieur *de la Sale* presented them with some
Knives and Bits of Tabacco, and they gave him
Bullocks Hides, very well dress'd with the Hair,
they gave one for a Knife, and would have given many more, but that we told to them,
that we had no Conveniency to carry them and
that if they had any Horses, he would give
them Axes in Exchange. They answer'd, they
had but two, which they could not part with.

It being late when Monſieur *de la Sale* return'd, *Feb.* 1687 we ſtaid there the reſt of the Day, and ſeveral *Indians* came to ſee us, in Hopes of receiving ſome Preſent, offering us Bullocks Hides dreſſed, which we would not burden our ſelves with.

The Second, we ſet out again, and halted ſome Time in that Village, where by the Way we barter'd for ſome Collars, or a Sort of Knots made of Bullocks Hides well dreſs'd, which the Natives make Uſe of to carry their Burdens, whether of Wood, Utenſils, or the Meat they kill. They prov'd of Uſe both to us and our Horſes, becauſe the Thongs of thoſe Collars ſerv'd to make faſt our Burdens.

We proceeded on our Journey, through a Country pleaſant enough, but Sandy, and hav- la Ma-ing croſs'd a large Plain, came to the Bank of ligne *Ri-*a fine River, call'd *la Maligne*, or the Miſchie- *ver.*vous, becauſe in Monſieur *de la Sale*'s former Journey, an Alligator devour'd one of his Ser-vants, who was ſwimming over it. This River is as wide as the *Seine* at *Roan*, ſeems to be very navigable and has a very pleaſant Country a-bout it. We incamp'd in a little Wood adjoin-ing to it, and bark'd the Aſpen Trees to hut.

Our Hunters kill'd Beeves, wild Goats, Tur-keys and other Wild-Fowl, and among the *Indian*reſt ſome Creatures as big as an indifferent Cat, *Rats.*very like a Rat, having a Bag under their Throat, in which they carry their Young. They feed upon Nuts and Acorns, are very fat, and their Fleſh is much like Pig.

Hard by there, we found a Place where Monſieur *de la Sale*, in his former Journey had hid ſome Parcels of Strings of Beads in the Trunks of Trees, and we reſted there till the Eighth of the Month During that Time, no

Day

Day pass'd without seeing some of the Natives, who sometimes spent the whole Day with us, and said they were of several Nations. We made them smoke, and always gave them some small Presents. They admir'd that after we had writ down some Words they spoke to us, we repeated them, looking on the Paper.

Portabl Canoe. Whilst we staid, Monsieur *de la Sale* set Men at Work to make a portable Canoe, of long Poles, hew'd and joyn'd and then cover'd with Bullocks Hides sew'd together, having pull'd off the Hair or Wooll, as it may be call'd there. That Canoe was of great Use to us, to cross Rivers as well for our selves as for our Baggage, but the Horses swam over.

The Ninth, we put our Canoe into the Water, and pass'd the River in it, and incamp'd half a League from thence, on Account of the Grass, which our Horses stood in Need of to recover themselves a little. The Tenth, we held on our Journey, crossing several spacious Plains, the Grass whereof was burnt, whence Monsieur *de la Sale* concluded, that there were many Natives thereabouts. He thought it convenient to provide Store of dry'd Flesh, for Fear we should not find Game in the Country we were going to enter upon, and accordingly caused several Beeves to be kill'd for that Purpose.

For that Reason, we continued there till the 12th, when we went and incamped on the Bank of a River, which Monsieur *de la Sale* had in his former Journey call'd *d'Eure*. At Night there arose a Storm, follow'd by Thunder and Rain, which swell'd the Streams, and obliged us to stay there. The 13th and 14th we cross'd four or five large Rivulets, and then a fine

curious

curious Country, diverfify'd with feveral little *Feb.* 1687
Woods, Hills and fmall Brooks, affording a delightful Profpect. That pleafant Country was
terminated by a Wood, which we were to crofs,
and were favour'd in it by a Way beaten by the
Bullocks, and at Night we incamped there.

The 15th, we travel'd along a fine Meadow,
then over Plains that had been burnt, and at
Night went to take our Reft on the Bank of a
fmall Rivulet, about which we faw feveral Foot-
fteps of Natives, which made us conclude we
were not far from them ; and therefore we
doubled our Guard, to prevent being furpriz'd.

The 16th, Monfieur *de la Sale* left me at the
Guard of the Camp, and took Monfieur *Cave-
lier* his Brother, and feven Men with him, to *A Village.*
go find out the *Indians.* They had not gone
half a League before they fpied Horfes and a
Number of Cottages, without being themfelves
feen by the Savages. That Village ftood on the
Side of a Hill, and contain'd about forty Huts,
ftanding together, befides feveral others ftragling.

When Monfieur *de la Sale* enter'd the Village,
the Savages feeing him, came to meet and con- *Monfieur*
duct him to the Cottage of their Chief, where *de la Sale*
he and his Company were feated on Bullocks *well re-*
Hides. The Elders being come, he fignify'd *ceiv'd by*
to them the Occafion of his Coming, as he had *the Na-*
done to the other Nations, with which they *tives.*
feem'd to reft fatisfy'd. Some Prefents were
made them, according to Cuftom, and they offer'd him a Quantity of Hides, which he refus'd, telling them, that when he return'd from
the *Cenis* he would trade with, and furnifh them
with all they had Occafion for. They confirm'd
what

what the others had told us, concerning a Nation, where some of them had been, the Men vvhereof were like us, meaning the *Spaniards*. He nam'd to them the Nations we had pass'd through from our Dwelling of St *Lewis*, to the River *Maligne*, which vve had lately pass'd. The Names of those Nations are as follows.

Names of
Nations
or Tribes.
The *Spicheats, Kabayes, Thecamons, Theauremets, Kiahoba, Choumenes, Kouans, Arhan, Enepiahe, Ahonerhopiheim, Korenkake, Korkone, Omeaoffe, Keremen, Ahehoen, Maghai, Thecamenes, Otenmarhem, Kavagan* and *Meracouman*. These are the Nations that lay on our Road ; those on the West and North West of the said River, were the *Kannehonan, Tohaka, Pehir, Coyabegux, Onapien, Pichar, Tohan, Kiaffes, Chanzes, Tfera, Bocrettes, Tfepehoen, Fercouteha, Panego, Petao, Petzares, Peifacho, Peihoum* and *Orcampion.*

Those we were with then, were call'd *Teao,* whom we had not before hear'd nam'd. They talk'd of a great Nation call'd *Ayona* and *Canohatino,* who were at War with the *Spaniards,* from whom they stole Horses, and told us, that one hundred *Spaniards* were to have come to join the *Cenis,* to carry on that War, but that having heard of our March, they went back. Monfieur *de la Sale* gave them to understand, that vve vvere at War vvith the *Spaniards,* and that we fear'd them not ; and that he was sent on their Account by the great Captain of the World, who had charg'd him to do them all Good, and to affist them in their Wars against such Nations as were their Enemies.

Those Savages gave Monfieur *de la Sale* Notice, that he would find three of our Men among the *Cenis,* which put him in Hopes they
were

were thofe he had given Leave to depart at his former Journey, and of whom he had never fince heard. He propos'd to them to barter for Horfes ; but they had caus'd them to be con-vey'd out of the Way, for Fear we fhould take them away, excepting only one Bay, which Monfieur *de la Sale* agreed for and return'd to us.

The 17th, we pafs'd a fmall River, with fome Difficulty, and incamp'd beyond it. The 18th, one of our Horfes going along the Edge of an upright Bank, fell into the Water, and came off with only a Hurt on the Shoulder ; but we were fain to unload him, and diftribute his Bur-den among us, every one making a Pack ; and thus we crofs'd a curious Plain, diverfify'd with Woods, Hills, Rivulets, and delightful Mea-dows.

The 19th, we travell'd along the Tops of thofe Hills, to avoid the Bottoms, and found a Difficulty to get down, by Reafon of the Rocks we met with at the End of them, and a River we were to crofs. Whilft we were paffing that River, we heard Dogs hunting the Bul-locks, two of which coming near us, one of them was fhot dead. The Natives who were hunting fpying us, fent out two of their Number, who creeping from Tree to Tree, drew near, and then ftood ftill, without daring to proceed any farther. We made Signs to them to come, which they did, and we made them fmoke, till Monfieur *de la Sale* return'd, being gone a little Way to obferve the Body of thofe People.

When come, he told them, he would enter-tain Peace with them, that we were going to
the

the *Cenis*, and he believ'd, that thefe very Men
were of their Nation, becaufe they had their
Accent and fome of their Words. They told
him their Village was near that Place, and bore
us Company to our Camp, where after fome
fmall Prefents given them, they were difmifs'd.

Account
given by a
Native.   The 20th, Monfieur *de la Sale* fent Monfieur
Moranget and fome others to the Village of
thofe Natives, to try whether they could barter with them for fome Horfes. In the mean
Time two Savages came to us, one of them being the fame that was with us the Night before,
and they exprefs'd much Friendfhip for us. That
particular *Indian* told us, his Name vvas *Pala-
quechaune*, that they were Allies to the *Cenis*,
that their Chief had been among the *Choumans*,
with the *Spaniards*; that the *Choumans* were
Friends to the *Spaniards*, from whom they got
Horfes, and added fome farther Particulars,
which the others had before fignify'd to us; fo
that vve had good Reafon to judge we vvere
not far from *North Mexico*.

He alfo told us, that the *Choumans* had given
their Chief fome Prefents, to perfwade him to
conduct us to them; that moft of the faid Nation had flat Heads; that they had *Indian* Corn,
which gave Monfieur *de la Sale* Ground to believe, that thofe People were fome of the fame
he had feen upon his firft Difcovery. That fame
Native had a very fine Goat's Skin, vvhich I
purchas'd of him for four Needles, after I had
fhewn him hovv to ufe them, and that Skin
vvas of good Ufe to make us Shoes inftead of
ravv Bullocks Hides.

is like Cod, and without Scales. The River sup- *Feb. 1686.*
ply'd us with Abundance of other Fishes, whose
Names we know not. The Sea afforded us
Oysters, Eeles, Trouts, a Sort of red Fishes
and others whose long, sharp and hard Beak
tore all our Nets.

We had Plenty both of Land and Sea Tor-
toises, whose Eggs serv'd to season our Sauces. *Tortoises.*
The Land Tortoises differ from those of the
Sea, as being smaller, round, and their Shell
more beautiful. They hide themselves in
Holes they find or make in the Earth. It
was looking for these Tortoises, that one of
our Surgeons, thrust his Arm into a Hole, and
was bit by some venomous Creature, which we
suppos'd to be a Sort of Toad, having four Feet,
the Top of his Back sharp and very hard, with
a little Tail. Whether it was this Crea- *Venomous*
ture, or a Snake, his Arm swelled very much, *Creatures.*
however he was cured by such Applications as
were made Use of; but it cost him a Finger
was cut off.

Among the venomous Sorts of Snakes, as
Vipers, Asps and others, whereof there are *Rattle-*
many, those call'd Rattle-Snakes are the most *Snakes.*
common. They generally lye among the Bram-
bles, where they make a Noise by the Motion
of two Scales they have at the End of their
Tail, which is heard at a considerable Distance,
and therefore they are call'd Rattle-Snakes.
Some of our Men had eaten of them and found
their Flesh was not amiss, and when we had
kill'd any of them, our Swine made a good
Meal.

There

There are alſo many **Alligators** in the Rivers, ſome of them of a frightful Magnitude and Bulk. I kill'd one that was between four and five Foot about, and twenty Foot in Length, on which our Swine feaſted. This Creature has very ſhort Legs, inſomuch that it rather drags along than walks, and it is eaſy to follow the Tract of it, either among the Weeds or on the Sands, where it has been. It is very ravenous, and attacks either Men or Beaſts, when they are within Reach in the River, and comes alſo aſhore to ſeek for Food. It has this particular Quality, that it flies from ſuch as purſue, and purſues thoſe who fly from it. I have ſhot many of them dead.

The Woods are compoſed of Trees of ſeveral Sorts. There are Oaks, ſome of them ever green and never without Leaves; others like ours in *Europe,* bearing a Fruit much like our Galls, and loſe their Leaves in Winter, and another Sort not unlike ours in *France,* but the Bark of them thicker, theſe as well as the ſecond Sort bear an Acorn, differing from ours both in Taſte and Bigneſs.

There is a Sort of Tree, which bears ſmall Berries, which, when ripe, are red, and indifferent pleaſant. It bears twice a Year, but the ſecond Crop never ripens. There is another Tree, bearing a Fruit not unlike *Caſſia,* in Taſte and Virtue.

There are others of the Sort I had ſeen in the Iſlands, whoſe Leaves are like Rackets, whence the Tree bears the Name. The Bloſſoms grow out about the Leaves, and of them comes a

Fruit ſomewhat reſembling Figs, but the Leaves and the Fruit are full of Prickles, which muſt
be

be carefully rubb'd and taken off, before it is
eaten, elfe they dangerously inflame the Mouth
and the Throat, and may prove mortal, as
happen'd to one of our Soldiers, who had eaten
of them too greedily, and without that Precau-
tion.

I have feen fome Trees refembling the Palm,
whofe lofty and long Branches fpread like that
call'd the *Latanier*, bearing a Fruit, faid to be indifferent good. Others the fame Sort, but whofe
Leaves are like Gutters, harfh and fo fharp
pointed, that they will pierce the thickeft Stuffs.
This Tree has a Sprout on the Top, which fhoots
out Flowers in the Shape of a Nofegay, of a
vvhitifh yellow, and fome of them at the Top
of that Sprout have fixty or eighty Flowers
hanging down, not unlike the Flower de Luce,
and after thofe Flowers follows a Fruit as long
as a Man's Finger, and thicker than the Thumb,
full of little Seeds, fo that there is fcarce any
Thing but the Rhind fit to eat, the Tafte
whereof is fweet and delicate

Vines. There are Abundance of creeping Vines
and others, that run up the Bodies and to the
Tops of Trees, which bear plenty of Grapes,
flefhy and fharp, not to compare to the Deli-
cacy of ours in *Europe*; but we made Verjuice
of them, which was very good in Sauce. Mulberry Trees are numerous along the Rivers,
their Fruit is fmaller, but fweeter and more
delicious than ours; their Leaves are beautiful
and large, vvhich would be of good Ufe for
feeding of Silkworms.

Plants. The Plains are ftrew'd with a Sort of fmall
Sorrel, the Leaf whereof is like Trefoil, and
the Tafte of it fharp like ours. There are A-
F   bundance

bundance of fmall Onions, no bigger than the Top of a Man's Finger, but very well tafted, and when the Heat has fcorch'd up the Plains, that Plant fhoots out firft, and produces Flowers, which look like an agreeable Enamel. Nothing is more beautiful than to behold thofe vaft Plains, when the Bloffoms appear ; a thoufand Sorts of different Colours, whereof many have an agreeable Scent, adorn thofe Fields, and afford a moft charming Object to the Eye. I have obferved fome that fmelt like a Tuberofe, but the Leaf refembles our Borage. I have feen Primrofes, having a Scent like ours, *African* Gilliflowers, and a Sort of purple wind Flowers. The Autumn Flowers are almoft all of them yellow, fo that the Plains look all of that Colour.

The Climate is mild and temperate, tho' we were in about 27 Degrees of North Latitude, and yet the Seeds I caufed to be fow'd did not thrive ; whether it was becaufe they had been foak'd in the Sea Water, or for any other Reafon. Some came up pretty well, as Pompions, Melons, Parfnips and Endive ; but the Beafts and the Infects, left us not much. When we come to the *Cenis* and have traverfs'd fo many Nations as lay between us and them, I fhall fpeak of the Religion, Manners, Cloathing, Houfes and Cuftoms of the Natives, wherin they differ but little from one another, tho' of feveral Countries.

Monfieur *de la Sale* had been now long gone, and we began to be in Pain for him, when about the Middle of *March* 1686, hapning to be on the Top of the Houfe, I fpied feven or eight Perfons coming towards us. I prefently ordered eight arm'd Men to follow me, to

go

go meet them; and as soon as we drew near them, we knew Monsieur *de la Sale*, Monsieur *Cavelier*, his Brother, Monsieur *Moranget*, his Nephew and five or six Men with them, the rest being gone another Way to find out the Bark *la Belle*, to give Notice of Monsieur *de la Sale*'s Arrival.

March 1686.

They were in a bad Condition, their Cloaths ragged, Monsieur *Cavelier*'s short Cassock hung in Tatters; most of them had not Hats, and their Linen was no better ; however the Sight of Monsieur *de la Sale* rejoyc'd us all. The Account he gave us of his Journey reviv'd our Hopes, tho' he had not found the fatal River, and we thought only of making ourselves as merry as we could. Only the Sight of the Sieur *Duhaut* interrupted it for some Time. Monsieur *de la Sale* ask'd me in an angry Manner, why I had receiv'd him, and *Duhaut* having given his Reasons, as I and my Men did, we were all satisfy'd.

Monsieur de la Sale returns.

The next Day, the Sieurs *le Barbier*, *Bihorel*, *le Petit*, *Cavelier*, the Nephew, the Surgeon and others, whom Monsieur *de la Sale* had sent to find out and carry Advice to the Bark *la Belle*, return'd, and said they could not find her, which was another fresh Cause of much Uneasiness to Monsieur *de la Sale*. He had been guilty of the Fault of putting aboard her, his Cloaths, his Linen, his Papers and all his best Effects, of all which he was then in the utmost Need. Besides, that Loss broke all the Measures he had concerted during his last Expedition, because he had resolv'd to cause the said Bark to go up one of the Rivers he had discover'd, to advance towards those Nations, with whom he had

The Bark la Belle lost.

F 2 con-

contracted ſome Friendſhip, and to ſend me in the ſame Bark, with his Nephew *Moranget*, to the Iſlands to ſeek for ſome Aſſiſtance, or elſe to return by Sea to look for his River.

All theſe Deſigns being diſappointed, he reſolv'd to ſet out a ſecond Time, and travel by Land, to find out his River. He ſtaid to reſt him a while, and to provide for his Departure, but having neither Linen nor Cloaths, I ſupply'd him with ſome I had ; I alſo afforded ſome Linen to Monſieur. *Cavelier*, his Brother and Monſieur *Moranget*, his Nephew. All I had was at their Service, and I depriv'd myſelf of all that was fit for them, even to ten or twelve Pounds of Strings of Beads and ſome Knives and Nails, which Monſieur *de la Sale* took.

The Sieur *Duhaut*, having ſeveral Effects, as Linen, Hatchets and other Tools and Commodities, which had been ſav'd from the Shipwreck, Monſieur *de la Sale* took Linen to make Shirts, for ſuch as wanted, as alſo the Tools they ſtood in Need of. The Cloaths belonging to Meſſieurs *Thibault*, *le Gros* and *Carpentier*, who were dead, were alſo diſtributed. A great Belt I had, ſerv'd to make Shoes for Monſieur *de la Sale* and Monſieur *Cavelier*.

All Things being thus provided, Monſieur *de la Sale* took twenty Men along with him, among whom were Monſieur *Cavelier* his Brother, F. *Anaſtaſius* a Recolet, Monſieur *Moranget* his Nephew, the Sieurs *Bihorel*, *le Clerk*, *Hurier*, *Duhaut* the younger, *Hiens* his Surgeon, and his Servants. He left behind thoſe, who were not fit to undertake that ſecond Journey, among whom were little Monſieur *Cavelier* his Nephew, the Sieur *Barbier*, *Canadien* and ſome others

Monſieur de la Sale ſets out upon another Expedition.

others. Each of the Travellers made up his *Apr.*1686
Pack, and they set out towards the latter End
of *April* 1686, after having given me the necessary Orders, and we parted without Ceremony,
Monsieur *de la Sale* desiring it should be so.

Some Days after he was gone, I heard a
Voice towards the lower Part of the River,
crying twice *Qui vive*, or who are you for. I
made that Way, and perceiv'd the Sieur *Chedeville* a Priest, the Sieur *de la Sablonniere*, and
some others of those who had been put aboard
the Bark *la Belle*, and were now in a Canoe. I
ask'd abruptly what was become of the Bark,
and was inform'd, our continual Misfortunes
still pursuing us, that it had run aground on the *What was*
other Side of the Bay. I caused the Canoe to *saved of*
be unloaded, there being in it, among other *the Bark*
Things, Monsieur *de la Sale*'s Cloaths, **Part** *la Belle.*
of his Papers, some Linen, a small Quantity of
Beads and thirty or forty Pound of Meal, which
was all they had left.

The next Day, Monsieur *de Chedeville* told
me the Particulars of that Misfortune, and said, *How the*
That having been some Time with the Bark, in *Bark was*
the Place where Monsieur *de la Sale* had ap- *lost.*
pointed them to wait, their Water falling short,
they had thought fit to send the Boat ashore,
with four or five Casks to fill; that the Sieur
Planterose went in it with six of the best Men.
That towards the Evening they saw the Boat
coming back, but the Wind being contrary and
Night coming on, they put out a Light, which
going out and the Captain neglecting to put up
another, in all Likelyhood the Boat could not
see the Bark, and they never heard of it after,

nor

nor of any of thoſe in it, who it was probable
had all periſh'd.

That nevertheleſs, they continued ſome Days
in the ſame Place, during which Time three or
four of their Men died ; and at laſt, having no
Water, they eat up their Swine, before they
died with Thirſt, and reſolv'd to weigh Anchor
and draw near to the Dwelling ; but having
few Hands and thoſe ſpent, and to add to their
Misfortune the Wind proving contrary, they
were drove to the other Side of the Bay, where
they run aground.

That having no Boat, nor Men enough to
land their Effects, they had endeavour'd to
make a Float with ſome Casks and Planks, but
that being ill made and join'd together, the
firſt that went upon it had periſh'd. That having made another Float better faſtned together
than the firſt, they had by that Means ſaved
ſome Sails and Rigging, ſeveral inconſidérable
Things, Linen, Cloaths and Papers belonging
to Monſieur *de la Sale* and others, and then
ſtay'd Aſhore, expecting to hear ſome News, and
had found a Canoe, being the ſame that was
before loſt on the Edge of the Bay, which had
been drove to the other Side ; and that Proviſions at laſt beginning to fall ſhort, they went
aboard the ſaid Canoe and came to us; fortunate in that they had not been diſcover'd by the
Natives, during their Stay Aſhore, which was
for the Space of three Months, and in finding
the Canoe to bring them back.

When Monſieur *de la Sale* went away, the
Sieur *Barbier* had taken upon him to go a hunting, as alſo to provide Bark to cover our Houſes, inſtead of Hides, becauſe the Sun drying
and

and contracting them, Part of the Top of our *June 1686*
Buildings was uncover'd. I farther enjoyn'd him
to cut Stakes, to make a Palisade about our
Dwelling, and the Sieur *Chedeville* having told
me they had bury'd several Things they could
not bring away, I sent the Sieur *Barbier* with
two Canoes and fifteen Men to the Place, where
they found some Pedreroes, Rigging and Sails.
The Natives having discover'd the Conceal-
ment, had taken away some Pieces of Linen
and Iron Tools, which they very much co-
vet.

The Sieur *Barbier* after his Return, continuing his Exercise of hunting, happen'd to meet
with a Parcel of the Natives, some of whom
had Firelocks, which they had taken from our *Encounter*
Men, and with which they made some Shots at *with the*
him, but very weak; and he firing three or four *Natives*
Shot at them they retir'd. He was then in a
Canoe on the River, and design'd to have gone
upwards; but that Rancounter having oblig'd
him to take another Way, and the Savages
perceiving it, eight of them swam over the River, hastening to get before the Canoe, hid
themselves among the Weeds, near the Way
he was to pass, and when he was near enough,
let fly their Arrows, which wounded several
Men. One Shot the Sieur *Barbier* made, put
them all to Flight again; he held on his Way
and return'd to our Habitation.

Some Days after, we perceiv'd a Herd of
Bullocks flying, and guess'd they were pursu'd
by the Savages, which afterwards appear'd to
be true. Some of them drew near to our Habitation, but a Cannon Shot, I pointed towards
the Gang of them, and a Musket-shot Mon-

sieur

ſieur *Barbier* fired at the neareſt, made them all fly farther off.

When the Sieur *Barbier* went out a Hunting, I commonly ſent with him ſome Women and Maids, to help the Hunters to dreſs and dry the Fleſh ; but being inform'd that he us'd to *The Sieur* ſlip aſide from the Company, with a young *Barbier* Maid he had a Kindneſs for, and which gave *marries.* Occaſion to ſome well-grounded Railleries ; the ſaid *Barbier* being told I was acquainted with that Affair, came and ſpoke to me in private, deſiring Leave to marry that young Woman, I made ſome Difficulty of it at firſt, adviſing him to ſtay till Monſieur *de la Sale* return'd ; but at laſt, conſidering they might have anticipated upon Matrimony, I took the Advice of the Recolet Fathers, and of Monſieur *Chedeville* the Prieſt, and allowed them to marry. Monſieur *le Marquis de la Sabloniere* following this Example, ask'd the ſame Liberty, being in Love with a young Maid, which I abſolutely refus'd, and forbid them ſeeing one another.

Some Time paſs'd in which Nothing happen'd to us worth obſerving ; however, I will mention two Things which befell our Recolet *Accidents* Fathers. One was, That Father *Anaſtaſius*, *concerning* being a hunting Bullocks with me, and coming *the Recolets* too near one I had ſhot, and was fallen, the Beaſt, as much hurt as he was, ſtarted up, attack'd and threw him down ; he had much ado to get off, and I to reſcue him, becauſe I durſt not ſhoot for Fear of killing him. The Bullock being weak, fell again ; the Father was deliver'd, but lay ill ſome Months. The other was, That Father *Maximus* had writ ſome Memoirs

moirs concerning Monſieur *de la Sale*'s Conduct,
condemning him upon ſeveral Occaſions. I was
told of it, found Means to get thoſe Memoirs,
threw them into the Fire, and ſo the Father
came off.

About the ſame Time, moſt of our Men
ſeeing Monſieur *de la Sale* did not return, began
to mutter. The Sieur *Duhaut*, who perhaps had
been the firſt Fomenter of thoſe Diſcontents,
back'd the Complaints of the diſguſted Party,
promis'd them great Matters under his Conduct, and offer'd to ſupply them with ſuch Effects as he had in Poſſeſſion, endeavouring, as I
ſuppoſe, by thoſe Means, to gain their Affecti-
ons, for a miſchievous Deſign, which it is likely
he had even then conceiv'd.

Duhaut Endea-vours to oc-caſion a Mutiny.

It was not long before, I had Intimation
of the whole Affair, and I had done Monſieur
de la Sale a ſingular Piece of Service, had I then
put to Death the Perſon, who was to be his
Murderer; but I reſted ſatisfy'd with giving
him a ſevere Reprimand, and threat'ning to
cauſe him to be ſecur'd if he perſiſted, being able
to do no other under my preſent Circumſtances. However, I talk'd to all concern'd, and
put them in ſuch Hopes of Monſieur *de la Sale*'s
Return, and that Things would ſoon change to
their Satisfaction, that they were all paci-
fy'd.

But in Regard, that Idleneſs often occaſions
Uneaſineſs and Impatience, I us'd all poſſible
Means to keep them employ'd, in the moſt o-
bliging Manner I could, ſetting ſome to cut
down the Buſhes about our Dwelling, others to
hew down Trees, that hinder'd the Proſpect, o-
thers mow'd the Graſs, that freſh might grow
up

June 1686   up for our Cattle, and at Night I made them divert themselves with Dancing and Singing.

M. de la Sale's *Discoveries.*   Whilst we thus pass'd away the Time the best we could, Monsieur *de la Sale* had penetrated very far up into the Country, inclining towards the Northern Part of *Mexico.* He had travell'd through several Nations, the Inhabitants whereof were, for the most Part, sociable, and had concluded a Sort of Alliance with them, and particularly with the *Cenis* and others whose Names I shall mention. He had discover'd charming Countries abounding in all Things that could be wish'd, as well for Sustenance, as for making of easy Settlements, and after he and his Nephew *Moranget* had escap'd two Dangerous Sicknesses, he return'd to our Habitation, with five Horses he had purchas'd, and arriv'd at it in *August* 1686.

His Return   Hearing of his Voice, I was one of the first that ran towards the River: We took our Canoes to bring him, his Luggage and some Provisions over, and the Horses swam. We were extraordinary glad to see our Commander in Chief return safe, tho' his Journey had not advanc'd his Design. Monsieur *de la Sale* had not found out his River, nor been towards the *Islinois* as we had hoped. Only eight Men return'd with him of twenty he carry'd out, and all the visible Advantage of that Journey consisted in five Horses, laden with Indian Wheat, Beans and some other Grain, which was put into the Store.

7 Men lost and 4 desert.   Monsr. *de la Sale* ask'd me, as soon as he came, whether the Sieurs *Clerc, Hurie, Duhaut* the younger and two others were come, because they

they not being able to endure the Fatigue of the Journey, he had given them Leave to return, and hearing they were not, he concluded the Savages had killed them. We were also inform'd, that the Sieur *Bihorel*, had ftray'd and was loft, fo that there had been no News of him fince ; that one of Monfr. *de la Sale*'s Servants had been dragg'd down to the Bottom of the Water and devour'd by an Alligator, and that four others had deferted and abandoned Monfieur *de la Sale*, when he was about the Country of the *Cenis*.

This was a very difmal and deplorable Account ; but the even Temper of our Chief made all Men eafy, and he found, by his great Vivacity of Spirit, Expedients, which reviv'd the loweft Ebb of Hope. He rejoiced at the Return and Sight of M. *Chedeville*, he was pleas'd at the Recovering of his Cloaths and Part of his Papers ; and after fome Time of Ref., he propos'd to undertake a Journey towards the *Iflinois*, and to make it the main Bufinefs, by the Way, to find the *Miffifipi* ; but it was thought proper to let the great Heats pafs, before that Enterptize was taken in Hand.

M. de la Sale refolves upa third Expedition.

In the mean Time, he gave Orders to ftake about a Place to make a new Magazine, or Storehoufe. He put to that Ufe the Timber I had caus'd to be cut, and would have more provided for the fame Ufe. Detachments being fent to work, feven or eight of our Men, who were fent with the Sieur *Barbier*, were difcover'd by the Savages, who being fuperior in Number, made as if they would hem them in ; but each of our Men having taken a Tree upon their Shoulders and fir'd their Pieces, which

made

Oct. 1686.

Two Men kill'd.

made one of the Natives drop, the others took him up and withdrew. Yet it was not long before they were reveng'd, for they kill'd us two Men, one of them clofe by our Dwelling, and the other, who had feparated from the reft of the Company to gather Purflain, and could not be reliev'd.

There being every Day fome Difcourfe of the Journey to the *Iflinois*, Monfieur *de la Sale* ask'd me one Day, whether I would make one of the Company, and go by the Way of *Canada* to *France* for Succours. I affured him I vvas entirely devoted to his Will, and vvould faithfully attend him. Then he began by Degrees to provide vvhat he thought neceffary for that Expedition. I had two Pair of Sheets, vvhich he took, to make him Linen. Canvas Cloaths vvere made of the Sails of the Bark *la Belle*. The Sieur *Duhaut* having Linen, he took fome to diftribute among feveral Perfons. Thus he hafted on the Execution of his Defign, but an Accident put it off.

*Nov.*1686

It vvas occafion'd by a Flux vvhich troubled Monfieur *de la Sale*, vvho having told me he could not perform that Journey, as long as he continu'd in fuch Condition, I offer'd to undertake it for him, if he vvould allow me his *Indian*, and about fifteen Men ; but he anfwer'd, That his Prefence was requifite among the *Iflinois*, and that it was requifite his Brother fhould go to *France*. Thus he refus'd my Offer, and could not fhun the ill Fate of that Journey.

*Dec.*1686

We fpent fome Time longer after this Manner, during the vvhich, there arofe a Controverfy about the Privileges the King grants to the Firft-born of the *French* Colonies in *Ameri-*

ca. The Sieur *Barbier*'s Wife vvas vvith Child, and he claim'd the Privilege granted for that Child. The Widow *Talon* had a Child born in the Paſſage from *France* to *America*, and alledg'd, that her Child, tho' born before our Arrival, ought to be preferr'd ; but the Sieur *Barbier*'s Wife miſcarrying, the Diſpute was not decided.

Monſieur *de la Sale* being recover'd of his Indiſpoſition, Preparations were again made for his Journey ; but we firſt kept the *Chriſtmas* Holy-Days. The Midnight Maſs was ſolemnly ſung, and on *Twelve-Day*, we cry'd, *The King drinks, (according to the Cuſtom of* France) tho' we had only Water: When that was over we began to think of ſetting out. Monſieur *de la Sale* gave the Command of the Settlement to the Sieur *Barbier*, directing him vvhat he vvas to do and obſerve in his Abſence.

There remain'd in that Habitation, the Fathers *Maximus* and *Zenobius*, Recolets, Monſieur *Chedeville*, the Prieſt, the Marquis *de la Sablonniere*, the Sieur *Barbier*, Commander, his Wife, a Surgeon and others, to the Number of twenty, among whom vvere ſeven Women, or Maids, and only the Sieur *Barbier* marry'd ; vvhich is much ſhort of the Number ſome have given out remain'd in the Dwelling, without any Ground ; for the Truth is, there vvere no more, and particularly no Natives, Monſieur *de la Sale* having abſolutely forbid holding any Communication vvith them. As for Beaſts, they amounted to ſeventy, or ſeventy five Swine, great and ſmall, vvhich vvas a good Stock ; for Fowl, eighteen or twenty Hens ; ſome Casks of Meal, vvhich

vvas

Jan.1687. vvas kept for the Sick; Powder, Ball, and eight Pieces of Cannon, vvithout any Bullets.

Perfons that fet out with M.de la Sale.   We fet out the 12th of *January*, in the Year 1687, being feventeen in Number, *viz.* Monfieur *de la Sale*, Monfieur *Cavelier*, the Prieft, his Brother, Father *Anaftafius*, the Recolet, Meffieurs *Moranget* and *Cavelien*, Nephews to Monfieur *de la Sale*, the Sieurs *Du-haut*, the Elder, *l' Arcleveque*, *Hiens*, *Liotot*, Surgeon, young *Talon*, an *Indian*, and a Footman belonging to Monfieur *de la Sale*, &c. We carried along vvith us Part of the beft Things every Man had, and vvhat vvas thought vvould be of Ufe, wherewith the five Horfes vvere loaded, and vve took our Leaves vvith fo much Tendernefs and Sorrow, as if vve had all prefaged, that vve fhould never fee each other more. Father *Zenobius* vvas the Perfon vvho exprefs'd it to me moft fignificantly, faying, He had never been fo fenfibly touch'd at parting with any Body.

The Way they travell'd.   We vvent that Day to the Place vve call'd *le Boucon*, becaufe there, vve had often dry'd Flefh, (*which the French call* Boucanner *from the Indian Word*) This Place was not far from our Habitation. The 13th, we crofs'd a Plain, about two Leagues over, where we faw feveral Herds of Beeves and Flocks of Goats, Turkeys, Buftards, and other Sorts of Wild Fowl. We met with Marfhy Lands, vvhich tired our Horfes, and came to a Wood that terminates the Plain, acrofs which, runs a Branch of a River, full of Reeds, by Monfieur *de la Sale* call'd the *Princefs's* River. That Branch joins the other, and they both fell together into the Bay of St. *Lewis*.

We

ſmall Bells; which making us look about, we ſpy'd
an *Indian* with a naked Sword-Blade in his Hand,
adorned with Feathers of ſeveral Colours, and
two large Hawks Bells, that occaſion'd the Noiſe
we had heard.

He made Signs for us to come to him, and
gave us to underſtand, that he was ſent by the
Elders of the Village, whither we were going,
to meet us, careſſing us after an extraordinary
Manner. I obſerv'd that it was a Spaniſh
Blade he had, and that he took Pleaſure in ring-
ing the Hawks Bells.

Having travell'd about half a League with him,
we diſcover'd a Dozen of other *Indians* coming *Kind Re-*
towards us, who made very much of and con- *ception.*
ducted us to the Village, to the Chief's Cottage,
where we found dry'd Bear-Skins laid on the
Ground, and they made us ſit on them, where
we were treated with Eatables, as were the
Elders after us, and a Throng of Women came
to ſee us.

The 7th, the Elders came to give us a Viſit,
bringing us two Bullocks Hides, four Otters Skins, *Preſents.*
one white Wild-Goat's Skin, all of them vvell
dry'd, and 4 Bows, in Return for the Preſent we
had before made them. The Chief and another
came again ſome Time after, bringing two
Loaves, the fineſt and the beſt we had yet ſeen.
They look'd as if they had been bak'd in an
Oven, and yet we had not obſerv'd, that there
were Ovens among any of them. That Chief
ſtay'd with us ſome Hours, he ſeem'd to be very
ingenious and diſcreet, and eaſily underſtood
our Signs, which vvere moſt of the Language
vve had. Having order'd a little Boy to bring
us all vve had Occaſion for, he vvithdrevv.

L   Tovvards

Towards the Evening, we were entertain'd with a Ceremony we had not seen before. A Company of Elders, attended by some young Men and Women came to our Cottage in a Body, singing as loud as they could roar. The foremost of them had a *Calumet*, so they call a very long Sort of Tabacco Pipe, adorn'd with several Sorts of Feathers. When they had sung a vvhile, before our Cottage, they enter'd it, still singing on, for about a Quarter of an Hour. After that, they took Monsieur *Cavelier* the Priest, as being our Chief, led him in solemn Manner out of the Cottage, supporting him under the Arms. When they were come to a Place they had prepared, one of them laid a great Handful of Grass on his Feet, two others brought fair Water in an Earthen Dish, with which they wash'd his Face, and then made him sit down on a Skin, provided for that Purpose.

When Monsieur *Cavelier* was seated, the Elders took their Places, sitting round about him, and the Master of the Ceremonies fix'd in the Ground two little wooden Forks, and having laid a Stick across them, all being painted red, he placed on them a Bullock's Hide, dryed, a Goat's Skin over that, and then laid the Pipe thereon.

The Song was begun again, the Women mixing in the Chorus, and the Concert was heightned by great hollow Calabashes or Gourds, in which there were large Gravel Stones, to make a Noise, the *Indians* striking on them by Measure, to answer the Tone of the Choir; and the pleasantest of all was, that one of the *Indians* plac'd himself behind Monsieur *Cavelier* to hold him

him up, whilst at the same Time he shook and *July* 1687
dandled him from Side to Side, the Motion
answering to the Musick.

That Concert was scarce ended, when the
Master of the Ceremonies brought two Maids,
the one having in her Hand a Sort of Collar, and
the other an Otter's Skin, which they plac'd on
the wooden Forks abovemention'd, at the Ends
of the Pipe. Then he made them sit down,
on each Side of Monsieur *Cavelier*, in such a Posture, that they look'd one upon the other, their
Legs extended and intermix'd, on which the
same Master of the Ceremonies laid Monsieur
Cavelier's Legs, in such Manner, that they lay
uppermost and across those of the two Maids.

Whilst this Action was performing, one of
the Elders made fast a dy'd Feather to the back
Part of Monsieur *Cavelier*'s Head, tying it to
his Hair. The Singing still continu'd all that
Time, so that Monsieur *Cavelier* grown weary
of its Tediousness, and asham'd to see himself
in that Posture between two Maids, without
knowing to what Purpose, made Signs to us to
signify the same to the Chief, and having given
him to understand, that he was not well, two
of the *Indians* immediately took hold of him
under the Arms, conducted him back to the
Cottage and made Signs to him to take his Rest.
This was about Nine in the Evening, and the
Indians spent all the Night in Singing, insomuch
that some of them could hold out no longer.

In the Morning they return'd to Monsieur
Cavelier, conducted him again out of the Cottage, with the same Ceremony and made him
sit down, still singing on. Then the Master of
the Ceremonies took the Pipe, which he fill'd

with

July 1687 with Tabacco, lighted and offered it to Monſieur *Cavelier*, but drawing back and advancing
ſix Times before he gave it him. Having at
laſt put it into his Hands, Monſieur *Cavelier*
made as if he had ſmok'd and return'd it to
them. Then they made us all ſmoke round,
and every one of them whiff'd in his Turn, the
Muſick ſtill continuing.

About Nine in the Morning, the Sun growing very hot, and Monſieur *Cavelier* being bare
Headed, made Signs that it did him Harm.
Then at laſt they gave over ſinging, and conducted him back into the Cottage, took the Pipe,
put it into a Caſe, made of a Wild-Goat's Skin,
with the two wooden Forks and the red Stick
that lay acroſs them, all which one of the Elders offer'd to Monſieur *Cavelier*, aſſuring him
that he might paſs thro' all the Nations that
were ally'd to them by Virtue of that Token of
Peace, and ſhould be every where well receiv'd.

Cahaync-
houa *Na-*
tion.
This was the firſt Place where we ſaw the *Calu-*
met, or Pipe of Peace, having no Knowledge of
it before, as ſome have writ. This Nation is
call'd *Cahaynohoua.*

Indians
expect Pre-
ſents.
This Sort of Ceremonies being never perform'd among the *Indians* without the Expectation of receiving ſome Preſent, and we having
beſides obſerv'd, that ſome of them had with-
drawn themſelves, with Tokens of Diſſatis-
faction, perhaps becauſe we had interrupted
their Ceremony, we thought it convenient to
give them ſomething more, and I was appointed to carry them an Ax, four Knives and ſome
Strings of Beads, with which they were ſatiſ-
fied.

We

We afterwards shew'd them an Experiment *July* 168**7** of our Arms, the Noise and Fire whereof frighted them. They earnestly press'd us to stay with them, offering us Wives and whatsoever else we should want. To be the better quit of them, we promis'd to return, saying we were going to fetch Commodities, Arms and Tools, which we stood in Need of, that we might afterwards stay with them.

The 9th and 10th were spent in Visits, and we were inform'd by one of the *Indians* that we were not far from a great River, which he describ'd with a Stick on the Sand, and shew'd it had two Branches, at the same Time pronouncing the Word *Cappa*, which, as I have said, is a Nation near the *Mississipi*. We then made no longer Question, that we were near what we had been so long looking after. We entreated the Elders to appoint some Men to conduct us, promising to reward them well, which they granted, and we set out the 11th, to the great Sorrow of those good People, who had entertain'd us so courteously.

We travell'd several different Ways, which we could never have found, had we wanted *The Jour-* Guides, and so proceeded till on the 12th, one of *ney prose-* our Guides pretended to be sick, and made *cuted.* Signs that he would go back; but observing, that we seem'd to be no Way concern'd, which we did on Purpose, he consulted with his Companion, and then came to tell us, he was recover'd. We made him eat and smoke, and continued our Journey the 13th, finding the Way very bad and difficult.

The

The 14th, our *Indians*, having feen the Track of Bullocks, fignify'd they would go kill fome, to eat the Flefh, which made us halt for two or three Hours. Whilft we ftay'd for our Hunters, we prepar'd fome *Sagamite*, or their Sort of Hafty-Pudding. They return'd loaded with Flefh, Part whereof we drefs'd, and eat it with very good Stomachs. Then we proceeded on our Journey till the 18th, and by the Way kill'd three Bullocks and two Cows, which oblig'd us to halt, that we might make ufe of our Flefh, drying it.

The Night between the 19th and the 20th, one of our Horfes breaking loofe, was either taken away by the Natives, or loft in the Woods. That did not obftruct our Departure, tho' the Lofs was grievous to us, and we held on our Way till the 24th, when we met a Company of *Indians*, with Axes, going to fetch Barks of Trees, to cover their Cottages. They were furpriz'd to fee us, but having made Signs to them to draw near, they came, carefs'd and prefented us with fome Water Melons they had. They put off their Defign of going to fetch Bark till another Time, and went along with us, and one off our Guides having gone before in the Morning to give Notice of our coming at the next Village, met with other Parcels of *Indians*, who were coming to meet us, and exprefs'd extraordinary Kindnefs.

Indians with Axes.

We halted in one of their Cottages, which they call *Defert*, becaufe they are in the Midft of their Fields and Gardens. There we found feveral Women who had brought Bread, Gourds, Beans and Water Melons, a Sort of Fruit proper
per

per to quench Thirſt, the Pulp of it being no better than Water.

We ſet out again to come to the Village, and by the Way, met with very pleaſant Woods, in which, there were Abundance of ſtately Cedars. Being come to a* River, that was between us and the Village, and looking over to the further Side,, we diſcover'd a great Croſs, and at a ſmall Diſtance from it, a Houſe, built after the *French* Faſhion.

A Croſs by a River and a French built Houſe

It is eaſy to imagine what inward Joy we conceiv'd at the Sight of that Emblem of our Salvation. We knelt down, lifting up our Hands and Eyes to Heaven, to return Thanks to the Divine Goodneſs, for having conducted us ſo happily; for we made no Queſtion of finding *French* on the other Side of the River, and of their being Catholicks, ſince they had Croſſes.

In ſhort, having halted ſome Time on the Bank of that River, we ſpy'd ſeveral Canoes making towards us, and two Men cloath'd, coming out of the Houſe we had diſcover'd, who, the Moment they ſaw us, fir'd each of them a Shot to ſalute us. An *Indian* being Chief of the Village, who was with them, had done ſo before, and we were not backward in returning their Salute, by diſcharging all our Pieces.

When vve had paſs'd the River, and vvere all come together, vve ſoon knew each other to be *French* Men. Thoſe we found vvere the Sieurs *Couture Charpantier* and *de Launay*, both of them of *Roan*, vvhom Monſieur *de Tonty*, Governor of Fort St. *Lewis* among the *Iſſinois*, had left at that Poſt, when he vvent down the *Miſ-*

Dwelling of French.

ſiſipi

July 1687. *fifipi* to look after Monfr. *de la Sale*; and the Nation vve vvere then vvith, vvas call'd *Accancea*.

It is hard to exprefs the Joy conceiv'd on both Sides ; ours was unfpeakable, for having at laft found, vvhat vve had fo earneftly *The Travellers come to the French Habitation.* defired, and that the Hopes of returning to our dear Country, was in fome Meafure affured by that happy Difcovery. The others vvere pleafed to fee fuch Perfons as might bring them News of that Commander, from vvhom they expected the Performance of vvhat he had promis'd them; but the Account vve gave them of Monfr. *de la Sale*'s unfortunate Death, vvas fo afflicting, that it drew Tears from them, and the difmal Hiftory of his Troubles and Difafters render'd them almoft inconfolable.

We vvere conducted to the Houfe, vvhither all our Baggage vvas honeftly carry'd by the *Indians.* There vvas a very great Throng of thofe People, both Men and Women, vvhich being over, vve came to the Relation of the particular Circumftances of our Stories. Ours vvas deliver'd by Monfieur *Cavelier*, vvhom vve honour'd as our Chief, for being Brother to him, who had been fo.

We vvere inform'd by them, that they had *Who the Frenchmen were.* been Six, fent by Monfr. *Tonty*, vvhen he return'd from the Voyage he had made down the *Colbert* or *Miffifipi* River, purfuant to the Orders fent him by the late Monfr. *de la Sale*, at his Departure from *France*, and that the faid Sieur *Tonty* had commanded them to build the aforefaid Houfe. That having never fince receiv'd any News from the faid Monfr. *de la Sale*

Sale, Four of them vvere gone back to Monſr. *July* 1687
Tonty, at the Fort of the *Iſlinois*.

In Concluſion, it vvas agreed among us, to go
away as ſoon as poſſible, towards the *Iſlinois*,
and conceal from the *Indians*, the Death of
Monſieur *de la Sale*, to keep them ſtill in Awe
and under Submiſſion, vvhilſt vve vvent away
vvith the firſt Ships that ſhould happen to ſail
from *Canada* for *France*, to give an Account at
Court of vvhat had happen'd, and to procure
Succours. In the mean Time, the Chief of the
Indians came to invite us to eat. We found
Mats laid on the Ground for us to ſit on, and
all the Village met to ſee us.

We gave them to underſtand, that we came
from Monſieur *de la Sale*, who had made a Settlement on the Bay of Mexico ; that we had
paſs'd thro' many Nations, which we nam'd,
and that we were going to *Canada* for Commodities, and would return down the River ; *Kind In-*
that we vvould bring Men to defend them a- *dians.*
gainſt their Enemies and then ſettle among
them ; that the Nations vve had paſs'd through
had appointed Men to guide us, and vve deſired
the ſame Favour of them, vvith ſome Canoes
and Proviſions, and that vve vvould reward
our Guides and pay for vvhat they furniſh'd
us.

The Conveniency of an Interpreter, vve then
had, gave us the Opportunity of making ourſelves be eaſily underſtood, and the Chief an-
ſvver'd to our Propoſals, that he vvould ſend
Men to the other Villages to acquaint them
vvith our Demands, and to conſult vvith them
vvhat vvas to be done in that Caſe ; that as
for the reſt, they vvere amaz'd at our having
paſs'd

pass'd thro' so many Nations, without having been detain'd, or kill'd, considering what a small Number we were.

When the Discourse was ended, that Chief caus'd Meat to be set before us, as dry'd Flesh, Bread made of *Indian* Corn of several Sorts, and Water Melons ; after which he made us smoke, and then we return'd to our House, where being eas'd of all those Impediments, we gave each other an Account of our Affairs, at Leisure, and were inform'd, that those People impatiently expected the Return of Monsieur *de la Sale*, which confirm'd us in the Resolution of concealing his Death. We observ'd the Situation of that Post, and were made acquainted with the Nature of the Country and the Manners of those People, of which I shall give the following Remarks.

French *House a-* *mong the* Acconcea's *described.* The House we were then in, was built of Pieces of Cedar laid one upon another, and rounded away at the Corners. It is seated on a small Eminency, half a Musket-shot from the Village, in a Country abounding in all Things. The Plains lying on one Side of it, are stor'd with Beeves, wild Goats, Deer, Turkeys, Bustards, Swans, Ducks, Teal and other Game.

Product of *the Coun-* *try.* The Trees produce plenty of Fruit, and very good, as Peaches, Plumbs, Mulberries, Grapes, and Wallnuts. They have a Sort of Fruit they call *Piaguimina*, not unlike our Medlars, but much better and more delicious. Such as live near the Rivers, as that House is, do not want for Fish of all Sorts, and they have *Indian* Wheat, whereof they make good Bread. There are also fine Plains diversify'd with several Sorts of Trees, as I have said before.

The

The Nation of the *Accancea's* confifts of four Villages. The firft is call'd *Otfotchove*, near which we were ; the fecond *Toriman*, both of them feated on the River ; the third *Tonginga* ; and the fourth *Cappa*, on the Bank of the *Miffi-fipi*. Thefe Villages are built after a different Manner from the others we had feen before, in this Point, that the Cottages, which are alike as to their Materials and Rounding at the Top, are long, and cover'd with the Bark of Trees, and fo very large, that feveral of them can hold two hundred Perfons, belonging to feveral Families.

The People are not fo neat as the *Cenis*, or the *Affonis* in their Houfes, for fome of them lie on the Ground, without any Thing under them but fome Mats, or a drefs'd Hide. However, fome of them have more Conveniencies, but the Generality has not. All their Moveables confift in fome Earthen Veffels and oval wooden Platters, which are neatly made, and with which they drive a Trade.

They are generally very well fhap'd and active ; the Women are handfome, or at leaft have a much better Prefence than thofe of the other Villages we pafs'd thro' before. They make Canoes all of one Piece, which are well wrought. As for themfelves they are very faithful, good natur'd, and Warriors like the reft.

The 25th, the Elders being affembled, came to fee us, and told the Sieur *Couture*, that they defign'd to fing and dance the *Calumet*, or Pipe ; becaufe the others had fung it, fome of them to the late Monfieur *de la Sale*, and the reft to Monfieur *Tonty*, and therefore it was but reafonable they fhould do the fame to get a Firelock,

lock, as well as the others. Monſieur *Cavelier*
was inform'd of it, and it was requiſite to con-
ſent to it, to pleaſe thoſe *Indians*, becauſe we
ſtood in need of them.

Ceremony   The Ceremony began with Monſieur *Cavelier*,
of the Pipe. who was led under the Arms and ſeated on a
Hide, without the Cottage. The Forks, the
Skins laid on it in Honour of the Pipe, the Singing as loud as they cou'd roar, both by Men
and Women, and all the other Ceremonies were
obſerv'd, as I have mention'd them before; ſo
that Monſieur *Cavelier* being weary of them, he
caus'd the Chief to be told, that he was out of
Order, and deſir'd his Nephew might be put in
his Place, which was done accordingly, and they
ſpent the whole Night in Singing. In the Morning they perform'd ſome other Ceremonies, not
worth relating.

The Solemnity being ended, by every Man's
ſmoking of the Pipe, the *Indians* took it, with
ſome Bullocks Hides, and Goats and Otters
Skins, and a Collar made of Shells, all which
they carry'd to our Houſe, and we gave them a
Firelock, two Axes, ſix Knives, one hundred
Charges of Powder, as much Ball, and ſome
Strings of Beads for their Wives. The Chief
having given Notice of our coming to the other
Villages, their Deputies came to ſee us; we entertain'd them in the Houſe, and propos'd to
them our Deſigns, as had been done to the
Chief. They ſtood conſidering a While, then
held a Sort of Conſultation among themſelves,
which held not long without talking, and then
agreed to grant us what we ask'd, which was a
Canoe and a Man of each Village to conduct us,
upon the promis'd Conſideration, and ſo they
went

went away to the Cottage of the Chief of the Village.

The 27th, the Chief and the Elders met again to confult about what we demanded of them; the Length of the Journey made them apprehenfive for thofe, who were to conduct us; but, at Length, we having difpell'd their Fears by our Arguments, and they having again deliberated fome Time, agreed to our Requeft. We again made them a Prefent, promifing a good Reward to our Guides, and fo we prepar'd to fet forwards. Little *Bartholomew* the *Parifian,* having intimated to us, that he would willingly ftay in that Houfe, becaufe he was none of the ableft of Body, we recommended him to the Sieur *Couture.* We defir'd thofe that remain'd there, to keep the Secret of Monfr. *de la Sale*'s Death, promis'd to fend them Relief, left them our Horfes, which were of great Ufe to go a Hunting, and gave them fifteen or fixteen Pounds of Powder, eight hundred Balls, three hundred Flints, twenty fix Knives, and ten Axes, two or three Pounds Weight of Beads; Monfr. *Cavelier* left them Part of his Linen, hoping we fhould foon be in a Place where we fhould get more; and all of them having made their Peace with God, by Means of the Sacrament of Penance, we took Leave of them, excepting the Sieur *Couture,* who went to conduct us Part of the Way.

The Journey continued.

We imbark'd on a Canoe belonging to one of the Chiefs, being at leaft twenty Perfons, as well Women as Men, and arriv'd fafe, without any Trouble, at a Village call'd *Toriman,* for we were going down the River. We propos'd it to thefe People, or rather demanded it

Toriman Village.

it of them to confirm what had been granted us by the others, and they referr'd giving us their Anſwer till the next Day ; for they do Nothing without conſulting about it, and we having brought a Sack of *Indian* Wheat, from the *French* Mens Houſe, deſir'd the Chief to cauſe Women to pound it, for which we would give em Something. Immediately he made a Sign to his Officers to go call them, and they went as readily.

There were ſeven or eight of thoſe Officers always about him, ſtark naked and beſmear'd, ſome after one Faſhion, and others after another. Each of them had three or four Calabaſhes or Gourds, hanging at a Leather Girdle

Officers. about their Waſtes, in which there were ſeveral Pebbles, and behind them hung a Horſe's Tail, ſo that when they ran, the Gourds made a ratling Noiſe, and the Tail being born up by the Wind, ſtood out at its full Length, ſo that Nothing could be ſeen more ridiculous ; but it behooved us to take Heed of ſhewing the leaſt Smile.

The remaining Part of the Day was ſpent in going with the Sieur *Couture* to ſee the fatal River ſo much ſought after by us, called

The River *Miſſiſipi* *found at* *laſt.* *Colbert,* when firſt diſcover'd, and *Miſſiſipi,* or, *Mechaſſipi* by the Natives that were near us. It is a very fine River and deep, the Breadth of it about a Quarter of a League, and the Stream very rapid. The Sieur *Couture* aſſur'd us, that it has two Branches or Channels, which parted from each other above us, and that we had paſs'd its other Branch, when we came to the firſt Village of the *Accancea's,* with which Nation we ſtill were.

The

The 28th, the Chief and the Elders being *July* 1687
assembled, they granted our Requests.   We
were to part, in order to be entertain'd in several Places, where we took Notice of some
particular Ceremonies, which we had not seen
among the other Nations.   One of them is, *Particular*
that they serve up their Meat in two or four *Ceremo-*
large Dishes, which are first set down before *nies.*
the two principal Guests, who are at one End,
and when they have eaten a little, those Dishes
are shov'd down lower and others are served
up in their Place, in the same Manner; so that
the first Dishes are serv'd at the upper End
and thrust down lower as others come in.

He who treats, does not sit down with the
Company, nor does he eat, but performs the
Part of a Steward, taking Care of the Dressing
and of the Placing of the Meat serv'd up; and
to the End he may appear the finer, he never
fails to besmear himself with Clay, or some red
or black Colouring they make use of.

The 29th, we set out from that Village, and
imbark'd on two Canoes to cross the *Mississipi:*
The Chief and about a Score of young Folks *Tonnin-*
bore us Company to the next Village call'd *Ton-* *guaVillage*
ningua, seated on the Bank of that River, where
we were receiv'd in the Chief's Cottage, as we
had been in the others.   The Elders treated
us in their Turns, and the Descriptions before
given will serve for this Place, there being but
little Difference between them and their Neighbours.

The 30th, we set out for *Cappa*, the last Vil- *Cappa*
lage of the *Accancea's*, eight Leagues distant from *Village.*
the Place we had left.   We were obliged to
cross the River *Mississipi* several Times in this
Way.

Way; becauſe it winds very much, and we
had ſome foul Weather, which made it late
before we could reach *Cappa*. A great Number of Youth came to meet us, ſome of them
conducted us to the Chief's Cottage, and others
took Care of our Baggage, which was reſtor'd
to us very honeſtly. We found the Elders
waiting for us; a great Fire was kindled to dry
us, and the Cottage was lighted by ſeveral
burning Reeds, which they make uſe of inſtead
of Flambeaus; after which we were ſerv'd as
in other Places.

The 31ſt. we receiv'd Viſits from the Elders.
Their Diſcourſe ran upon the War they deſign'd
to make, thinking to ingage us in it, and we
return'd the ſame Anſwer as we had done to
the others, that we would ſoon return with all
Things we ſtood in Need of. We ask'd a Man
of them, which was granted, and the Day ended in Feaſting.

Entertain-
ment given
by the Indi-
ans.
We would willingly have ſet out the Firſt
of *Auguſt*; but the Chief came and told us, it
could not be, becauſe the Women had not
pounded our Corn, which however was done;
but they made uſe of that Pretence to oblige us
to ſtay, and to have Leiſure to give us ſome
Diverſion, after their Manner. Accordingly,
about Ten in the Morning, the Warriors and
Youth came together to Dance. They were
dreſs'd after their beſt Manner, ſome of them
wearing Plumes of ſeveral Colours, wherewith
they adorn their Heads, others, inſtead of Feathers, had two Bullocks Horns, and were all
beſmear'd with Clay, or Black and Red, ſo that
they really look'd like a Company of Devils or
Monſters, and in thoſe Figures they danc'd,
as

as I have defcrib'd it, fpeaking of the other *Aug.* 1687
Nations.

The Second, we made ready to be going.
The *Indian* given by the firft Village for our
Guide, would not go any farther. A Man,
faid to be an Hermaphrodite, offer'd to fupply
his Place, faying, he was willing to go to the
Iflinois. We took Leave of the Sieur *Couture*,
to whom Monfr. *Cavelier* made an Exhortati-
on, encouraging him to perfevere and have Patience, in Hopes of the Relief we wou'd fend
him, and fo we imbark'd on the *Miffifipi* in a
Canoe, being Nine in Number, that is, five of
us, and the four *Indians* that were our Guides.
We were oblig'd to crofs that River very often, and no lefs frequently to carry our Canoe
and Goods, as well on Account of the Rapidi-
ty of the River, and to find it flacker on the
one or the other Side of it, which was very
troublefome to our Guides, as becaufe of the
little Iflands we met with, which are form'd
by the impetuous beating of the Water upon
the Banks, that oppofe its Courfe, where the
Channels happen not to lie ftrait ; there it
wafhes away the Earth and bears down great
Trees, which in Procefs of Time form little
Iflands, that divide the Channel. At Night
we incamp'd in one of thofe fmall Iflands, for
our greaterSafety,for we were then come into an *Machiga-*
Enemy's Nation, call'd *Machigamea*, which put *mea Nati-*
our *Indians* into great Frights. *on.*

It is certain our Toil was very great, for we
were oblig'd to row in the Canoe, to help our
Indians to ftem the Current of the River, becaufe we were going up, and it was very
ftrong and rapid ; we were often neceffitated

to land, and ſometimes to travel over miry Lands, where we ſunk up half way the Leg; other Times over burning Sands, which ſcorch'd our Feet, having no Shoes, or elſe over Splinters of Wood, which ran into the Soles of our Feet, and when we were come to the reſting Place, we were to provide Fuel to dreſs our Meat, and provide all Things for our *Indians,* who would not have done ſo much as go fetch a Cup of Water, tho' we were on the Bank of the River, and yet we were happy enough in having them.

We proceeded on, continually undergoing the ſame Toil, till the Seventh, when, we ſaw the firſt Bullock, we had met on our Way, ſince our coming among the *Accancea's.* The *Indians,* who had a great Mind to eat Fleſh, made a Sign to me, to go kill it. I purſu'd and Shot, but it did not fall, the *Indians* ran after, kill'd, and came to tell us it muſt be parch'd, or dry'd, which was accordingly done. I muſt here take Notice of a Ceremony our *Indians* perform'd, when they came near the Bullock, before they flead him.

Ceremony at dreſſing a Bullock. In the firſt Place, they adorn'd his Head with ſome Swans and Buſtards Down, dy'd red, and put ſome Tabacco into his Noſtrils, and between the Clefts of the Hoofs. When they had flead him, they cut out the Tongue, and put a Bit of Tabacco into its Place; then they ſtuck two Wooden Forks into the Ground, laid a Stick acroſs them, on which they plac'd ſeveral Slices of the Fleſh, in the Nature of an Offering. The Ceremony being ended, vve parch'd or dry'd the beſt Parts of the Beaſt and proceeded on our Journey.

The

The 9th, vve found the Banks of the River very high, and the Earth of them Yellow, Red and White, and thither the Natives came to furnish themſelves with it, to adorn their Bo- dies, on Feſtival Days. We held on our Way till the 14th, vvhen vve met a Herd of Bul- locks, whereof we kill'd five, dry'd Part of them, and proceeded till the 18th.

The 19th, we came to the Mouth of the River, call'd *Houabache*, ſaid to come from the Country of the *Iroquois*, towards *New England*. That is a very fine River, its Water extraor- dinary clear, and the Current of it, gentle. Our *Indians* offer'd up to it, by Way of Sacrifice, ſome Tabacco and Beef Steaks, which they fix'd on Forks, and left them on the Bank, to be diſ- pos'd of as the River thought fit. We obſerv'd ſome other Superſtitions among thoſe poor Peo- ple, one whereof was as follows.

There were ſome certain Days, on which they Faſted, and we knew them, when aſſoon as they awak'd, they beſmear'd their Faces and Arms, or other Parts of their Bodies, with a ſlimy Sort of Earth, or pounded Charcoal; for that Day they did not eat till Ten or Eleven of the Clock at Night, and before they did eat they were to vvipe off that Smearing, and had Water brought them for that Purpoſe. The Occaſion of their Faſting was, as they gave us to underſtand, that they might have good Succeſs in Hunting, and kill Abundance of Bul- locks.

We held on our Way till the 25th, when the *Indians* ſhew'd us a Spring of Salt Water, within a Musket Shot of us, and made us go aſhore to view it. We obſerv'd the Ground

about

Aug. 1687 about it was much beaten by Bullocks Feet, and it is likely they love that Salt Water. The *WildFruit.* Country about, was full of Hillocks, cover'd vvith Oaks and Wallnut-Trees, Abundance of Plum-Trees, almoft all the Plums red and pretty good, befides great Store of other Sorts of Fruits, whofe Names vve know not, and among them one fhap'd like a midling Pear, with Stones in it as big as large Beans. When ripe it peels like a Peach, the Tafte is indifferent good, but rather of the Sweeteft.

The 27th, having difcover'd a Herd of Beeves, we went afhore to kill fome ; I fhot a Heifer, which was very good Meat, we put a Board the beft of it, and held on our Way till the Evening, when we encamp'd on an Ifland, where we obferv'd an Alteration in the Humour and Behaviour of our *Indians.* This put us under fome Apprehenfion, and the more, for that he who was reckon'd an Hermaphrodite, told us, they intended to leave us, which oblig'd us to fecure our Arms and double our Watch during the Night, for Fear they fhould forfake us.

With that Jealoufy we proceeded on our Journey the 28th and 29th, coafting along the Foot of an upright Rock, about fixty, or eighty Foot high, round which the River glides. Held on the 30th and 31ft, and the firft of *Septem-* *Miffouris ber* pafs'd by the Mouth of a River call'd *Mif-* *River.* *fouris,* whofe Water is always thick, and to which our *Indians* did not forget to offer Sacrifice.

Figure of The 2d, we arriv'd at the Place, where the *a pretend-* Figure is of the pretended Monfter fpoken of by *ed Monfter* Father *Marquet.* That Monfter confifts of two

                                                        fcurvy

ſcurvy Figures drawn in red, on the flat Side of a Rock, about ten or twelve Foot high, which wants very much of the extraordinary Height that Relation mentions. However our *Indians* paid Homage, by offering Sacrifice to that Stone; tho' we endeavour'd to give them to underſtand, that the ſaid Rock had no Manner of Virtue, and that we worſhip'd ſomething above it, pointing up to Heaven; but it was to no Purpoſe, and they made Signs to us, that they ſhould die if they did not perform that Duty. We proceeded, coaſting along a Chain of Mountains, and at length, on the 3d, left the *Miſſiſipi*, to enter the River of the *Iſſi-* *nois.*

We found a great Alteration in that River, as well with Reſpect to its Courſe, which is very gentle, as to the Country about it, which is much more agreeable and beautiful than that about the great River, by Reaſon of the many fine Woods and Variety of Fruit its Banks are adorn'd with. It was a very great Comfort to us, to find ſo much Eaſe in going up that River, by Reaſon of its gentle Stream, ſo that we all ſtay'd in the Canoe and made much more Way.

Thus we went on till the 8th, without ſtopping any longer than to kill a Bullock, and one of our *Indians*, who had a craving Stomach, having eaten ſome of its Suet hot and raw, was taken very ill, and died of it, as I ſhall mention in its Place.

The 9th, we came into a Lake, about half a League over, which we croſs'd, and return'd into the Channel of the River, on the Banks whereof we found ſeveral Marks of the Natives

having

having been incamp'd there, when they came to fiſh and dry what they caught. The 10th, we croſs'd another Lake, call'd *Primitehouy*, return'd to the River, and the 11th, ſaw *Indians* before us, incamp'd on the Bank of a River, whereupon we ſtop'd and made ready our Arms. In the mean Time, one of them came towards us by Land, and we put on our Canoe towards him.

Meeting with Iſſinois.

When that *Indian* was near, he ſtood gazing on us, without ſpeaking a Word, and then drawing ſtill nearer, we gave him to underſtand, that we were ſent by Monſieur *de la Sale*, and came from him. Then he made Signs to us, to advance towards his People, whom, he went before to acquaint with what we had ſaid to him, ſo that when we were come near them they fired ſeveral Shot to ſalute us, and we anſwer'd them with our Firelocks.

After that mutural Salutation, they came into our Canoe, to ſignify, they were glad to hear News of Monſieur *de la Sale*. We ask'd them, What Nation they were of; they anſwer'd, They were *Iſlinois*, of a Canton call'd *Caſcaſquia*. We enquir'd whether Monſieur *Tonty* was at Fort *Lewis* ; they gave us to underſtand, that he was not, but that he was gone to the War againſt the *Iroquois*. They invited us Aſhore, to go with them to eat of ſuch as they had, we thank'd them, and they brought us ſome Gourds and Water Melons, in Exchange for which, we gave them ſome parch'd Fleſh.

We had not by the Way taken Notice of a Canoe, in which was a Man with two Women, who, being afraid of us, had hid themſelves

felves among the Reeds, but that Man feeing us *Sept.* 1687
ftop among his Countrymen, took Heart, came
to us, and having told us, that he belong'd to a
Village near **Fort** *Lewis*, we fet out together,
and one of our *Indians* went into that Canoe,
to help them to fhove, fo they call the Way of
pufhing on the Canoe with Poles inftead of
rowing.

On *Sunday*, the 14th of *September*, about two *Fort Lew-*
in the Afternoon, we came into the Neigh- *is among*
bourhood of Fort *Lewis*. Drawing near, vve *the* Illinois
were met by fome *Indians* that were on the
Bank, who having view'd us well, and underftanding we came from Monfr. *de la Sale*, and
that we belong'd to him, ran to the Fort to
carry the News, and immediately we faw a
French Man come out, with a Company of *Indians*, who fir'd a Volley of feveral Pieces, to fa-
lute us. Then the *French* Man drew near, and
defir'd us to come Afhore, which we did, leaving only one in the Canoe, to take Care of our
Baggage; for the *Iflinois* are very fharp at carrying off any thing they can lay their Hands
on, and confequently, nothing near fo honeft
as the Nations we had pafs'd thro'.

We all walk'd together towards the Fort,
and found three *French* Men coming to meet us,
and among them a Clerk, who had belong'd to *Arrival at*
the late Monfr. *de la Sale*. They immediately *Fort Lewis*
ask'd us, where Monfr. *de la Sale* was, we told
them, he had brought us Part of the Way, and
left us at a Place about forty Leagues beyond
the *Cenis*, and that he was then in good Health.
All that was true enough; for Monfr, *Cavelier*
and I, who were the Perfons, that then fpoke,
were not prefent at Monfr. *de la Sale*'s Death;

M 4 he

he was in good Health when he left us, and I have told the Reaſons we had for concealing his Death, till we came into *France*.

It is no leſs true, that Father *Anaſtaſius*, and he they called *Teiſier*, could have given a better Account, the one as an Eye Witneſs, and the other, as one of the Murderers, and they were both with us ; but to avoid lying, they ſaid Nothing. We farther told them, we had Orders to go over into *France*, to give an Account of the Diſcoveries made by Monſieur *de la Sale*, and to procure the ſending of Succours.

At length, we enter'd the Fort, where we found and ſurpriz'd ſeveral Perſons who did not expect us. All the *French* were under Arms
and made ſeveral Diſcharges to welcome us. Monſieur *de Belle Fontaine* Lieutenant to Monſr. *Tonty*, was at the Head of them and complimented us. Then we were conducted to the Chappel, where we return'd Thanks to God, from the Bottom of our Hearts, for having preſerv'd and conducted us in Safety ; after which we had our Lodgings aſſign'd us, Monſr. *Cavelier* and Father *Anaſtaſius* had one Chamber, and we were put into the Magazine, or Ware-houſe. All this While, the Natives came by Intervals, to fire their Pieces, to expreſs their Joy for our Return, and for the News we brought of Monſieur *de la Sale*, which refreſh'd our Sorrow for his Misfortune ; perceiving that his Preſence would have ſettled all Things advantageouſly.

The Day after our Arrival, one of the *Indians*, who had conducted us, having been ſick ever ſince he eat the raw Beef Suet, I mention'd before, died, and his Companions took away
and

and bury'd him privately. We gave them the promis'd Reward, and the Part belonging to the Dead Man, to be deliver'd to his Relations. They ſtay'd ſome Time in the Fort, during the which, we took extraordinary Care of them, and at laſt they return'd to their own Homes.

As far as we could gather by half Words dropp'd there by one or other at the Fort, Something had been done there prejudicial to the Service of Monſr. *de la Sale*, and againſt his Authority, and therefore ſome dreaded his Return, but more eſpecially a *Jeſuit* was in great Conſternation. He was ſick, Monſieur *Cavelier*, Father *Anaſtaſius* and I went to viſit him. He enquired very particularly of all Points, and could not conceal his Trouble, which we would not ſeem to take Notice of.

Our Deſign being to make the beſt of our Way to *Canada*, in Order to ſet out Aboard the firſt *French* Ships that ſhould Sail for *France*, we enquired how we were to proceed, and met with ſeveral Difficulties. The Navigation on that River was very dangerous, by Reaſon of *Falls in the River.* the Falls there are in it, which muſt be carefully avoided, unleſs a Man will run an inevitable Hazard of periſhing. There were few Perſons capable of managing that Affair, and the War with the *Iroquois* made all Men afraid.

However the Sieur *Boiſrondet*, Clerk to the late Monſr. *de la Sale*, having told us he had a Canoe, in which he deſign'd to go down to *Canada*, we prepared to make uſe of that Opportunity. Care was taken to gather Proviſions

visions for our Voyage, to get Furs to barter as we pass'd by *Micilimaquinay*. The Visits of two Chiefs of Nations, call'd *Cascasquia Peroueria* and *Cacahouanous* discover'd by the late Monsieur *de la Sale*, did not interrupt our Affairs, and all things being got ready, we took Leave of those we left in the Fort. Monsieur *Cavelier* writ a Letter for Monsieur *Tonty*, which he left there to be delivered to him, and we repair'd to the Lake to imbark.

It would be needless to relate all the Troubles and Hardships we met with, in that Journey, it was painful and fruitless, for having gone to the Bank of the Lake, in very foul Weather, after waiting there five Days, for that *M. Cave-* foul Weather to cease, and after we had *lier, &c.* imbark'd, notwithstanding the Storm, we were *set out and* oblig'd to put Ashore again, to return to the *returns* Place where we had imbark'd, and there to dig *again.* a Hole in the Earth, to bury our Baggage and Provisions, to save the Trouble of carrying them back to Fort *Lewis*, whither we return'd and arrived there the 7th of *October*; where they were surpriz'd to see us come back.

Thus were we oblig'd to continue in that Fort all the rest of *Autumn* and Part of the *Winter*, to our great Sorrow, and not so much for our own Disappointment, as for being, by that Means, obstructed from sending of Succours, as soon as we had expected, as well to the said Fort, as to those *French* of our own Company, whom we had left on the Coast of the Bay of *Mexico*,

It

It was then the good Seaſon for ſhooting. *Oct.* 1687
Thoſe Gentlemen at the Fort had ſecur'd two
good *Indian* Sportſmen, who never let us want
for Wild Fowl of all Sorts; beſides we had
good Bread, and as good Fruit, and had there
been any Thing to drink beſides Water, we had
far'd well. The Leiſure we had during our
Stay there, gave me an Opportunity of making
the following Remarks, as well of my own Obſervation, as what I learn'd of the *French* re-
ſiding there.

Deſcrip-
tion of Fort
Lewis and
the Country
about it.

Fort *Lewis* is in the Country of the *Iſlinois*
and ſeated on a ſteep Rock, about two hundred
Foot high, the River running at the Bottom of
it. It is only fortified with Stakes and Paliſades,
and ſome Houſes advancing to the Edge of the
Rock. It has a very ſpacious Eſplanade, or
Place of Arms. The Place is naturally ſtrong,
and might be made ſo by Art, with little Expence. Several of the Natives live in it, in
their Huts. I cannot give an Account of the
Latitude it ſtands in, for Want of proper Inſtruments to take an Obſervation, but Nothing
can be pleaſanter ; and it may be truly affirm'd,
that the Country of the *Iſlinois* enjoys all that
can make it accompliſh'd, not only as to Ornament, but alſo for its plentiful Production of
all Things requiſite for the Support of human
Life.

The Plain, which is water'd by the River, is
beautified by two ſmall Hills, about half a
League diſtant from the Fort, and thoſe Hills
are cover'd with Groves of Oaks, Walnut-
Trees and other Sorts I have named elſewhere.
The Fields are full of Graſs, growing up very
high. On the Sides of the Hills is found a
gravelly

Lime and
Clay for
Bricks, &c.

Oct. 1687 gravelly Sort of Stone, very fit to make Lime for Building. There are also many Clay Pits, fit for making of Earthen Ware, Bricks and Tiles, and along the River there are Coal Pits, the Coal whereof has been try'd and found very good.

Mines. There is no Reason to question, but that there are in this Country, Mines of all Sorts of Metals, and of the richest, the Climate being the same as that of *New Mexico.* We saw several Spots, where it appeared there were Iron Mines, and found some Pieces of it on the Bank of the River, which Nature had cleansed. Travellers who have been at the upper Part of the *Mississipi,* affirm they have found Mines there, of very good Lead.

Product. That Country is one of the most temperate in the World, and consequently whatsoever is sow'd there, whether Herbs, Roots, *Indian* and even *European* Corn thrives very well, as has been try'd by the Sieur *Boisrondet,* who sow'd of all Sorts, and had a plentiful Crop, and we eat of the Bread, which was very good. And whereas we were assured, that there were Vines which run up, whose Grapes are very good and delicious, growing along the River, it is reasonable to believe, that if those Vines were transplanted and prun'd, there might be very good Wine made of them. There is also Plenty of wild Apple and Pear Trees, and of several other Sorts, which would afford excellent Fruit, were they grafted and transplanted.

All other Sorts of Fruit, as Plumbs, Peaches and others, wherewith the Country abounds, would become exquisite, if the same Industry were

were us'd, and other Sorts of Fruit we have in *Oct.* 1687
France would thrive well, if they were carry'd
over. The Earth produces a Sort of Hemp,
whereof Cloth might be made and Cordage.

As for the Manners and Cuftoms of the *Ifli-* *Manners*
nois, in many Particulars they are the fame as *and Cuftoms of*
thofe of the other Nations we have feen. They *the Ifli-*
are naturally fierce and revengeful, and among *nois.*
them the Toil of Sowing, Planting, carrying
of Burdens, and doing all other Things that *Women do*
belong to the Support of Life, appertains pe- *all Labour.*
culiarly to the Women. The Men have no o-
ther Bufinefs but going to the War and hunting, and the Women muft fetch the Game
when they have kill'd it, which fometimes they
are to carry very far to their Dwellings, and
there to parch, or drefs it any other Way.

When the Corn or other Grain is fow'd,
the Women fecure it from the Birds till it comes
up. Thofe Birds are a Sort of Starlings, like
ours in *France*, but larger and fly in great
Swarms,

The *Iflinois* have but few Children, and are *Children.*
extreamly fond of them ; it is the Cuftom a-
mong them, as well as others I have mentioned, never to chide, or beat them, but only to
throw Water at them, by Way of Chaftife-
ment.

The Nations we have fpoken of before, are *Thieving.*
not at all, or very little, addicted to Thieving ;
but it is not fo with the *Iflinois*, and it behoves
every Man to watch their Feet as well as their
Hands, for they know how to turn any Thing
out of the Way moft dexteroufly. They are
fubject to the general Vice of all the other *In-*
dians, which is to boaft very much of their *Boafting.*
\Warlike

Oƌ. 1687. WarlikeExploits,and that is the main Subject of their Diſcourſe, and they are very great Lyars.

Care of the Dead. They pay a Reſpect to their Dead, as appears by their ſpecial Care of burying them, and even of putting into lofty Coffins the Bodies of ſuch as are conſiderable among them, as their Chiefs and others, which is alſo practiſed among the *Accancea's*, but they differ in this Particular, that the *Accancea's* weep and make their Complaints for ſome Days, whereas the *Chahouanous* and other People of the *Iſlinois* Nation do juſt the Contrary ; for when any of them die, they wrap them up in Skins, and then put them into Coffins made of the Barks of Trees, then ſing and dance about them for twenty four Hours. Thoſe Dancers take Care to tie Calabaſhes, or Gourds about their Bodies, with ſome *Indian*Wheat in them,to rattle and make aNoiſe, and ſome of them have a Drum, made of a great Earthen Pot, on which they extend a wild Goat's Skin, and beat thereon with one Stick, like our Tabors.

Preſents to the Dead. During that Rejoicing, they throw their Preſents on the Coffin, as Bracelets, Pendants, or Pieces of Earthen Ware, and Strings of Beads, encouraging the Singers to perform their Duty well. If any Friend happens to come thither at thatTime, he immediately throws down his Preſent and falls a ſinging and dancing like the reſt. When that Ceremony is over, they bury the Body, with Part of the Preſents, making choice of ſuch as may be moſt proper for it. They alſo bury with it, ſome Store of *Indian* Wheat, with a Pot to boil it in, for fear the dead Perſon ſhould be hungry on his long Journey ;

and

and they repeat the fame Ceremony at the *Oct. 1687.* Year's End.

A good Number of Prefents ftill remaining, *Game of* they divide them into feveral Lots, and play at *the Stick.* a Game, call'd of the Stick, to give them to the Winner. That Game is play'd, taking a fhort Stick, very fmooth and greas'd, that it may be the Harder to hold it faft. One of the Elders throws that Stick as far as he can, the young Men run after it, fnatch it from each other, and at laft, he who remains poffefs'd of it, has the firft Lot. The Stick is then thrown again, he who keeps it then has the fecond Lot, and fo on to the End. The Women, whofe Husbands have been flain in War, often perform the fame Ceremony, and treat the Singers and Dancers whom they have before invited.

The Marriages of the *Iſlinois* laft no longer, *Marriages* than the Parties agree together; for they freely part after a HuntingBout, each going whichWay they pleafe, without any Ceremony. However, the Men are jealous enough of their Wives, and when they catch them in a Fault, they generally cut of their Nofes, and I faw one who had been fo ferv'd.

Neverthelefs, Adultery is not reckon'd any *Adultery.* great Crime among them, and there are Women who make no Secret of having had to do with *French* Men. Yet are they not fufficiently addicted to that Vice to offer themfelves, and they never fall, unlefs they are fued to, when, they are none of the moft difficult in the World to be prevail'd on. The reft I leave to thofe who have liv'd longer there than I.

VVe

Oet. 1687.

How the Travellers liv'd.

We continu'd ſome Time in Fort *Lewis,* without receiving any News. Our Buſineſs was, after having heard Maſs, which we had the good Fortune to do every Day, to divert our ſelves the beſt we could. The *Indian* Women daily brought in ſomething freſh, we wanted not for Water Melons, Bread made of *Indian* Corn, bak'd in the Embers, and other ſuch Things, and we rewarded them with little Preſents in Return.

M. Tonty *comes to* Fort Le-wis.

On the 27th of *October,* of the ſame Year, Monſieur *Tonty* return'd from the War with the *Iroquois.* Our Embraces and the Relation of our Adventures were again repeated ; but ſtill concealing from him , the Death of Monſieur *de la Sale.* He told us all the Particulars of that War, and ſaid, That the *Iroquois* having got Intelligence of the March of the *French* Forces and their Allies, had all come out of their Villages and laid themſelves in Ambuſh by the Way ; but that having made a ſudden and general Diſcharge upon our Men, with their uſual Cries, yet without much Harm done, they had been repuls'd with Loſs, took their Flight, and by the Way burnt all their own Villages. That Monſieur *d' Hennonville,* chief Governor of *New France,* had cauſ'd the Army to march, to burn the reſt of their Villages, ſet Fire to their Country and Corn, but would not proceed any farther. That afterwards he had made himſelf Maſter of ſeveral Canoes belonging to the *Engliſh,* moſt of them laden with Brandy, which had been plunder'd ; that the *Engliſh* had been ſent Priſoners to *Montreal,* they being come to make ſome Attempt upon the *Iſinois,*

War with the Iro-quois.

We

We continued after this Manner, till the *Dec.*1687. Month of *December*, when two Men arrived, from *Montreal*. They came to give Notice to Monſr. *Tonty*, that three Canoes, laden with Merchandize, Powder, Ball and other Things, were arriv'd at *Chicagon*, that there being too little Water in the River, and what there was being frozen, they could come down no lower; ſo that it being requiſite to ſend Men to fetch thoſe Things, Monſr. *Tonty* deſir'd the Chief of the *Chahouanous* to furniſh him with People. That Chief accordingly provided forty, as well Men as Women, who ſet out with ſome *French* Men. The Honeſty of the *Chahouanous* was the Reaſon of preferring them before the *Iſlinois*, who are naturally Knaves.

That Ammunition and the Merchandize were *Feb.*1688. ſoon brought, and very ſeaſonably, the Fort being then in Want. We ſtay'd there till the End of *February*, 1688, at which Time we fix'd our Reſolution to depart, tho' we had no News from *Canada*, as we expected. We found there were ſome Canoes ready to undertake that Voyage, and we laid hold of that Opportunity to convoy each other to the *Micilimaquinay*, where we hop'd to meet ſome News from *Canada*.

Monſieur *Cavelier* the Prieſt, had taken Care, before the Death of M. *de la Sale*, his Brother, to *Mar.*1688 get of him a Letter of Credit, to receive either a Sum of Money or Furs in the Country of the *Iſlinois*. He tender'd that Letter to M. *Tonty*, who believing M. *de la Sale* was ſtill alive, made no Difficulty of giving him to the Value of about 4000 Livres in Furs, Caſtors and Otter Skins, a Canoe and other Effects, for which, the ſaid

N

Monſr.

*Mar.*1688 Monſr. *Cavelier* gave him his Note, and we prepar'd for our Journey.

I have before obſerved, that there was a *Jeſuit*, whoſe Name was *Dalouez* at Fort *Lewis*,
and who had been very much ſurpriz'd to hear
that Monſr. *de la Sale* was to come in a ſhort
Time, being under great Apprehenſions on
Account of a Conſpiracy intended to have been
carry'd on, againſt Monſr. *de la Sale*'s Intereſt.
That Father perceiving our Departure was
fix'd, mov'd firſt, and went away foremoſt,
to return to *Micilimaquinay*; ſo that they
were left without a Prieſt at Fort *Lewis*, which
was a great Trouble to us, becauſe we were the
Occaſion of it, and therefore thoſe, who were
to remain in the Fort, anticipated the Time,
and made their *Eaſter*, taking the Advantage of
the Preſence of F. *Anaſtaſius* and M. *Cavelier*.

At length, vve ſet out the 21th of *March*,
from Fort *Lewis*. The Sieur *Boiſrondet*, who was
deſirous to return to *France*, join'd us, we imbark'd on the River, which was then become
navigable, and before we had advanc'd five
Leagues, met with a rapid Stream, which oblig'd
us to go Aſhore, and then again into the Water,
to draw along our Canoe. I had the Misfortune to hurt one of my Feet againſt a Rock
that lay under Water, which troubled me very much for a long Time; and we being under
a Neceſſity of going often into the Water, I
ſuffer'd extreamly, and more than I had done
ſince our Departure from the Gulph of *Mexico*.

We arriv'd at *Chicagon* the 29th of *March*, and
our firſt Care was to go ſeek vvhat vve had
conceal'd at our former Voyage, having, as
was there ſaid, bury'd our Luggage and Proviſions.

*The Travel
continued.*

88 We took Leave of the *Jesuits*, and set out in four Canoes, *viz.* two belonging to Monsieur *de Porneuf*, and two to Monsieur *Cavelier*, one of which had been brought from Fort *Lewis*, and the other bought, as I have just now said, vve being twenty nine of us in those four Canoes. We row'd on till the 24th, when Monsieur *de Porneuf* left us to go to St. *Mary*'s Fall, to carry the Orders given him. The 25th, we got out of the Lake of the *Islinois*, to enter that of the *Hurons*, on the Banks whereof stands the Village, call'd *Tessalon*, where Monsieur *de Porneuf* came again to us, with a Canoe of the Natives, and with him we held on our Way.

We proceeded to *Chebonany* the 30th of *June*, and the 3d of *July*, enter'd the *French* River, where we were forc'd several Times to carry our Canoes to avoid the Falls and the rapid Streams, observing as we went a barren and dry Country, full of Rocks, on which there grew Cedars and Fir Trees, which take Root in the Clefts of those Rocks.

The 5th, we enter'd upon the little Lake of *Nipicingue*, adjoining to a Nation of that Name. We got out of it again and enter'd upon the great River, where, after having pass'd the great Fall, we arriv'd the 13th, at the Point of the Island of *Montreal*. We landed at a Village call'd *la Chine*, which had belong'd to the late Monsr *de la Sale*. Monsr. *Cavelier* set out the 14th, for *Montreal*, where we came to him the 17th.

At *Montreal* we found the Marques d' *Hennonville*, Monsieur *de Noroy* the Intendant and other

sions. We found it had been open'd, and some Furs and Linen taken away, almost all which belong'd to me. This had been done by a *French* Man, whom M. *Tonty* had sent from the Fort, during the Winter Season, to know whether there were any Canoes at *Chicagon*, and whom he had directed to see whether any Body had medled with what we had conceal'd, and he made Use of that Advice to rob us.

Mar. 1688

The bad Weather oblig'd us to stay in that Place, till *April*. That Time of Rest was advantageous for the Healing my Foot; and there being but very little Game in that Place, we had Nothing but our Meal or *Indian* Wheat to feed on; yet we discover'd a Kind of *Manna*, which was a great Help to us. It was a Sort of Trees, resembling our Maple, in which we made Incisions, vvhence flow'd a sweet Liquor, and in it we boil'd our *Indian* Wheat, which made it delicious, sweet and of a very agreeable Relish.

Sweet Water from a Tree.

There being no Sugar-Canes in that Country, those Trees supply'd that Liquor, which being boil'd up and evaporated, turn'd into a Kind of Sugar somewhat brownish, but very good. In the Woods we found a Sort of Garlick, not so strong as ours, and small Onions very like ours in Taste, and some Charvel of the same Relish as that we have, but different in the Leaf.

The Weather being somewhat mended, vve imbark'd again and enter'd upon the Lake on the 5th of *April*, keeping to the North Side to shun the *Iroquois*. We had some Storms also, and saw swelling Waves like those of the Sea; but arriv'd safe the 15th at a River call'd *Quinetonan*, near a Village whence, the Inhabitants depart during the Winter Season, to go a Hunting, and reside there all the Summer.

Quinetonan River.

The

Apr. 1688   The Sport is not there as in thofe Countries from whence we came; but on the Contrary, very poor, and we found Nothing but fome very lean Wild Goats, and even thofe very rarely, becaufe the Wolves, which are very numerous there, make great Havock of them, taking and devouring great Numbers after this Manner.

How Wolves catch Goats   When the Wolves have difcover'd a Herd of Wild Goats, they roufe and fet them a running. The Wild Goats never fail to take to the firft Lake they meet with.   The hunting Wolves, who are ufed to that, guard the Banks carefully, moving along the Edges of them. The poor Goats being pierc'd by the Cold of the Lake, grow weary and fo get out, or elfe the River fwelling forces them out with its Waves, quite benumm'd, fo that they are eafily taken by their Enemies, who devour them. We frequently faw thofe Wolves watching along the Side of the Lake, and kept off to avoid frightning them, to the End the Wild Goats might quit their Sanctuary, that we might catch fome of them, as it fometimes fell out.

Pou'oua-tanni Nation.   The 28th, we arriv'd among the *Poutouatannis*, which is half Way to *Micilimaquinay*, where we purchas'd fome *Indian* Corn for the reft of our Voyage. We found no News there from *Montreal*, and were forc'd to ftay fome Time to wait an Opportunity to go down the River. No Man daring to venture, becaufe of the War with the *Iroquois*.

Hurons and Outa-houacs Nations.   There are fome *French* Men in that Place, and four *Jefuits*, who have a Houfe well built with Timber, inclofed with Stakes and Palifades. There are alfo fome *Hurons* and

and *Outahouacs*, two Neighbou whom thofe Fathers take Care without very much Trouble, thof downright Libertines, and there none but a few Women in th Thofe Fathers have each of thei of inftructing a Nation, and to th tranflated the proper Prayers into peculiar to each of them, as al Things relating to the Catholick F ligion.

They offer'd Father *Anaftafius* a *Cavelier* a Room, which they acce we took up our Lodging in a little Travellers had made. There we c reft of *May* and Part of *June*, till aft of *Whitfontide*. The Natives of t about, till the Land and fow *Indian* lons and Gourds, but they do not thr as in the Country we came from. they live on them, and befides they they catch in the Lake, for Flefh is v among them.

On the 4th of *June*, there arriv'd fo commanded by Monfieur *de Porneuf*, co *Montreal*, and bringing News from th *d' Hennonville*, and Orders to fend to tlements which were towards the Lake and others higher up, towards the the River *Colbert*, to know the Pof Condition of Affairs. We prepar'd tc with the two Canoes. Monfieur *Cavelic* another, to carry our Baggage, and of his Furs with a Merchant, who gav Note to receive Money at *Montreal.* fame with thofe few Furs I had, the reft having been left at *Micilimaquinay*,

other Gentlemen, to whom we gave an Account of our long and painful Travels, with the Particulars of what we had seen, which they listned to with Satisfaction, but without mentioning Monsieur *de la Sale*'s Death. We told them the Occasion of our going over into *France*, and they approv'd of it, being of Opinion with us, that we ought to hasten our Departure as much as possible.

We made us some Cloaths, whereof we stood in Need. The Sieur *Teissier*, who came along with us, and was of the Reform'd Religion, knowing the Exercise of it was forbid in *France*, abjur'd it in the great Church of *Montreal*.

The 27th, we went aboard a Bark to go down the River to *Quebec*, where we arriv'd the 29th, Father *Anastasius* carry'd us to the Monastery of the Fathers of his Order, seated half a League from the Town, on a little River, where we were most kindly receiv'd by the Father Guardian and the other Religious Men, who express'd much Joy to see us, and we still more for being in a Place of Safety, after so many Perils and Toils, for which we return'd our humble Thanks to Almighty God, our Protector.

We chose rather to take up our Lodging there than in the Town, to avoid the Visits and troublesome Questions every one vvould be putting to us with much Importunity, which vve must have been oblig'd to bear patiently. Monsieur *Cavelier* and his Nephew, vvhom vve had left at *Montreal*, arriv'd some Days after us, and vvere lodg'd in the Seminary.

We

We ftay'd in that Monaftery till the 21ft of *Auguft*, when we imbark'd on a large Boat, eighteen Perfons of us, to go down the River of *St. Laurence*, a Board a Ship, that was taking in and fifhing of Cod. We went a Board it the 30th of the fame Month, and after hearing Mafs, made ready and fail'd for our dear Country, arriv'd fafe at *Rochelle* on *Saturday* the 9th of *October* 1688, whence, fetting out · by Land, the 15th, the fame Providence, which had protected and conducted us, brought us without any Misfortune to *Roan*, the 7th of *October*, the fame Year.

The End of the J O U R N A L.

The Remainder of the L E T T E R, *written by him who revis'd this* J O U R N A L, *the other Part whereof is at the Beginning of it, this being the* Sequel *to the faid* J O U R N A L.

Note, *That thefe have writ of thofe Parts, but none of this particular Voyage.*

T H R E E feveral Authors have given an Account of this Voyage; *Firft*, Father *le Clerk*, upon the Relations he had from the Fathers *Zenobius* and *Anaftafius*, Recolets, as he was himfelf and both of them Eye-Witneffes : *Secondly*, The Chevalier *Tonty*, who was alfo a Witnefs to a confiderable Part of thofe Adventures : And, *Laftly*, Father *Hennepin*, a *Flemming,*

ming, of the fame Order of the Recolets, has done it more largely, he feems to be well acquainted with the Country, and had a great Share in thofe Difcoveries; but the Truth of his Relations is much controverted. It was he who went to the Northward, and towards the Source of the *Miſſiſipi*, which he calls *Mechaſipi*, and who printed, at *Paris*, an Account of the Country about the River, giving it the Name of *Louiſiana*. He ought to have ftopp'd there, and not to have gone, as he did, into *Holland*, to fet forth another Edition, very much enlarg'd, and perhaps not fo true, which he dedicated to *William* the Third, Prince of *Orange*, and afterwards King of *Great Britain*. An Action for a Religious Man no lefs ridiculous than extravagant, not to give it a worfe Name; for after many great and tedious Encomiums given that Proteftant Prince, he, exhorts and conjures him to turn his Thoughts towards thofe vaft Countries, as yet unknown, to conquer them and fend Colonies thither, to make known to thofe Savage Nations the true God and his Worfhip, and to preach the Gofpel. That good Religious Man, whom many have falfly thought, on Account of that Extravagancy, to have renounc'd his Religion, did not confider what he faid, and confequently has fcandaliz'd the Catholicks, and furnifh'd the *Hugonots* with Matter of Laughter; for is it likely, that they being Enemies to the *Roman* Church, would employ Recolets to go preach up *Popery*, as they call it in *Canada* ? Or would they introduce any other Religion than their own? Can Father *Hennepin* be excufeable in this Point?

In

In fine it appears, by all that has been writ by those several Persons concerning that Enterprize, that the Murder committed on the Person of Monsieur *de la Sale* was the Occasion of its miscarrying; but that which obstructed the making of some Provision in that Case was, the said Murders being conceal'd for the Space of two Years, and that the *Spaniards* of *Mexico* having been inform'd of all the Affair, sent

M. de la Sale's *Fort taken by the* Spaniards.

Men, who carry'd off the weak Garrison Monsieur *de la Sale* had left in the Fort built by him, near the Place of his Landing, before he penetrated into the Country, to find out the *Missisipi*. They also entirely raz'd that Fort, so that Seven or Eight Years elaps'd, till Monsieur *de Hiberville*, a Gentleman of *Canada*, and a Person of Capacity and Courage, famous for his notable Exploits in *Hudson*'s Bay and other Parts, resolv'd to reassume and revive that Project. He came over into *France* upon that Design, and made an Armament about the Year 1698, set out and sail'd to the Gulf of *Mexico*.

M. de Hiberville's *Expedition for the* Missisipi.

Being an able Seaman, he search'd along the Coast so narrowly, that he found the Mouth of that fatal *Missisipi* and built a Fort on it, leaving Men there, with a good Quantity of Ammunition and Provisions, and return'd to *France*, intending to go back with a Reinforcement, as he did, and having penetrated far into the Country, discover'd several Savage Nations, and join'd Friendship and Alliance with them, as also built another Fort, which he left well stor'd with Men and Necessaries, return'd into *France*; but attempting a third Voyage, he dy'd by the Way, and thus, for want of Relief and

Sup-

Support, that noble Enterprize miscarry'd again.

But God has now provided for it, and it is the Concern of Heaven, for if *France* is interested on Account of the Temporal Advantages it expects, the Church is so in like Manner, for the Conversion of the *Indians* it hopes will follow. Accordingly, Providence has taken the Affair in Hand, having rais'd the Man, who is the fittest to revive and support so important a Project. This is Monsieur *Crozat*, Secretary to the King, a Man of singular Worth, very Intelligent, Well-meaning, and prodigiously Rich, who without going out of his Closet, has been the Occasion of many notable Voyages by Sea, and all of them successful. To him, his Majesty, by his Letters Patent, bearing Date the 14th of *Septemb.* 1712. has granted the sole Power to trade and settle Colonies in the Countries describ'd in this Journal, and which are known to us by the Name of *Louisiana* and the River *Missisipi*, from hence forward to be call'd the River of St. *Lewis*. The Grant is made to him for 15 Years, under several Conditions mention'd in the said Letters-Patent, which have been made publick.

M. Crozat only to plant Colonies and Trade in Louisiana.

And whereas such a Grant cannot subsist without Blacks, he is also allow'd to send a Ship to *Guinea* to purchase them. They may perhaps find there the famous Black *Aniaga*, Brother to a King of *Guinea*, whom Captain *Delbee* brought over into *France*, above Thirty Years ago. The King was pleas'd to have him Educated, Instructed and Baptiz'd, the *Dauphin* being his Godfather; then put him into his Troop of Musquetiers, and afterwards made him

him a Captain in his own Regiment, where he
serv'd Honourably. Being desirous to see his
own Country again, where he promis'd to pro-
mote the *French* Trade, and the settling of Missioners, his Majesty loaded him with Presents, and order'd a Ship to carry him back to
Guinea ; but as soon as he was there, he no longer remember'd he had been baptiz'd, and
turn'd again as perfect a Black, as he had been
before. A Friend of mine, who was an Officer
aboard a Ship, and hapned to be on that Coast
in the Year 1708, had two or three Interviews
with that Black, who came aboard him. He
was a great Man in that Country, for his Brother was King. He express'd much Gratitude
for the Kindness that had been shewn him in
France, and was extraordinary Courteous, and
made great Offers to those aboard the Ship, and
to all such of the Nation as would go into
Guinea.

A Black bred in France turns to his Native Customs.

This Navigation to *Louisiana* will farther procure us a free Resort to the two famous Ports
of the Gulf of *Mexico*, viz. The *Havana* and
Veracruz, where Strangers did not use to be admitted, and which we knew only by their Names
and their Situation in our Maps.

Veracruz in New Spain.

The latter of those Towns is the Port of
New Spain, at the Bottom of the Bay or Gulf,
in 18 Degrees of *North* Latitude, Seated in a
Sandy Plain, encompass'd with Mountains ; beyond which there are Woods and Meadows,
well Stock'd with Cattle and wild Fowl. The
Air is very Hot, and not Healthy, when any
Winds blow, except the *North*, which rises
commonly once in Eight or Fifteen Days, and
holds for the Space of Twenty Four Hours,
blowing

blowing fo hard, that there is no going afhore from the Ships, and then the Cold is very piercing. When the Weather is clear there plainly appear, on the Road to *Mexico*, two Mountains rifing above the Clouds, and forty Leagues diftant, all cover'd with Snow. The Streets of *Veracruz* are ftreight as a Line; the Houfes are handfome and regular; the Fortifications next the Land inconfiderable, but the Front of the Town next the Sea forms a Semicircle, with a little Fort at each End. Directly before that Front, a Quarter of a League out at Sea, there ftands, on a Spot of Ground, inacceffible, by Reafon of the Breaking of the Sea, a ftrong Citadel, well built and furnifhed with all Neceffaries, a good Garrifon and double Batteries of two hundred Pieces of brafs Cannon. Ships cannot anchor any where, but between that Citadel and the Town; befides that, it requires feveral Precautions, becaufe it is difficult coming to an Anchor.

Moft of the Inhabitants are *Mulattoes*, that is of a tawny dark Colour, who live moft upon Chocolate and Sweetmeats, extraordinary fober, and eating little Flefh. The Men are haughty, the Women keep retired above Stairs, not to be feen by Strangers, and feldom going abroad, and then in Coaches or Chairs, and thofe who cannot reach to it, cover'd with fine filk Veils, which reach from the Crown of their Heads to their Feet, leaving only a fmall Opening on the Right Side, for them to fee their Way. In their own Apartments they wear nothing but a Smock and a filk Petticoat, with gold or filver Laces, without any Thing on their Heads, and

and their Hair platted with Ribbons, a gold Chain about their Neck, Bracelets of the same and Pendants of Emeralds in their Ears. They could well enough like the Behaviour and Company of the French, but that the jealous Temper of the Men obstructs them. There being a Picture of *Philip* King of *Spain*, now reigning, aboard the Ship in which my Friend was, who gave me this Account, the People swarm'd aboard to see it, they were never satisfy'd with gazing at it, and there was a most magnificent Festival kept in the Town, on Account of the Birth of the Prince of *Asturias*.

They understand Trade very well, but are sloathful and averse to Labour, fond of State and Ease. They wear great Strings of Beads about their Necks, their Houses are full of Pictures and Images of Devotion, decently furnish'd with Purceline and *China* Goods. The Churches are magnificently adorned with Plate.

All Strangers are forbid Trading there, yet some come by Stealth and deal Underhand, by Means of Presents made to such Persons as can favour them. If those Mulattoes call themselves white, it is only to honour themselves and by Way of Distinction from their Slaves, who are all Blacks, and having got much Mony by their Labour, ransome themselves and sometimes become considerable Merchants.

Mexico City.

The City of *Mexico*, Capital of the Country and the Residence of the Vice-roy, is about eighty Leagues distant from *Veracruz*, to the Westward, the Way to it very bad and ill furnish'd with Provisions. That Country would be better in some Parts, were it well cultivated

cultivated by the Inhabitants. They fow but little of our Wheat, and are fatisfied with *Indian* Corn and *Caſſabi* Root, whereof they make Cakes, as is practis'd in the Iſlands. Their Trees and Fruits are the fame as in other hot Countries. About the Town of *Veracruz*, there are Buſhes of a Sort of Thorn, without Leaves, among which grows an extraordinary Plant; for tho' it has but a ſmall Stem, it ſhoots out Leaves of a Cabbage Green, as thick as a Man's Finger, which grow out, one at the End of another, in the Shape of a Racket, and the Plant itſelf is ſo call'd. From thoſe Leaves there grows out a Sort of red Figs, very juicy, with Seeds like thoſe of the Pomgranate; the Juice is of a Violet Colour, but unſavoury. There is a Sort of Flies that cleave to it and are ſo fond of the Taſte of the Fruit, that they burſt and drop down dead. They are carefully gather'd and dry'd, and are the Scarlet Dye, call'd *Cochinilla*, which is brought into *Europe*, and makes that beautiful Colour. The Birds and Beaſts are much the fame as in other Countries of *America*. There is a Sort of Bird, all red, which for that Reaſon is call'd the *Cardinal*; this they often tame and teach to ſing like a *Canary* Bird. This is what I have been told concerning the Town of *Veracruz*.

As for the *Havana*, a Town and Port no leſs famous, in the Iſland of *Cuba*, belonging as well as the other to the Crown of *Spain*, it ſtands towards the Weſtern End, and on the North Side of that Iſland, almoſt under the Tropick of *Cancer*, and about four or five hundred Leagues on this Side of *Veracruz*. It is large and beautiful

Havana,

ful

ful; the Port good, secur'd by two Forts on the two Sides, and Brass Guns, from twenty four to thirty six Pounders, the Entrance so narrow, that only one Vessel can go in at once. The Town is encompass'd by a good Wall, fortify'd with five Bastions, furnish'd with Cannon. The Streets are all as strait as a Line, and level, the Houses very handsome, but ill furnish'd. In the Midst of it is a fine Square, the Buildings about all uniform. The Churches are magnificent, and enrich'd with Gold and Silver, Lamps, Candlesticks, and Ornaments for the Altars. There are some Lamps curiously wrought, which weigh two hundred Marks of Silver, each Mark being half a Pound. The Revenue of the Bishoprick amounts to fifty thousand Crowns, and he who enjoy'd it in the Year 1703, as I was inform'd by my Friend, who gave me this Account of what he had seen, was the greatest Ornament of that City, for his Virtues and Charity, being satisfy'd with Necessaries, and spending all the rest upon the Poor, and in repairing decay'd Churches. Tho' Strangers are prohibited to trade there, yet it is easier carried on than at *Veracruz*. The Inhabitants are more familiar; the Women have more Liberty, yet they do not go Abroad without their Veils to wrap and hide them. Many of them speak *French*, and dress after the *French* Fashion, and some of our Nation have settled themselves there. When my Friend was there, a magnificent Festival was celebrated for fifteen Days successively, in Honour of K. *Philip* the Fifth, and Monsieur *du Casse* being then there, with his Squadron, the City desir'd him to join with them. To that Purpose, he set

ashore

aſhore five hundred Men, who perform'd the
Martial Exerciſe in the great Square, which
was much admir'd. The *Havana* is the Place,
where the Galeons meet. Proviſions are dear
there, eſpecially Bread ; but the Wine is not,
tho' it is good. Fiſh and Fleſh there, are un-
ſavory. The Inhabitants are *Spaniards.*

We have thought fit to deſcribe thoſe two
famous Ports of the Bay of *Mexico,* as well becauſe it has not been ſo exactly done before, as
in Regard that the Settlement which is going
to be made in *Louiſiana,* may have ſome De-
pendance on them ; for the *Havana* lying in the
Way, thoſe who perform the Voyage may have
the Conveniency of taking in Refreſhments
there, of putting in for Shelter in foul Weather, and of careening or refitting. As for the
Veracruz, tho' farther out of the Way, the
Correſpondence there may be advantagious for
the Securing of the Colony of *Louiſiana.*

But how can that fail of ſucceeding, under
the Conduct of Monſieur *Crozat,* who has the
Charge of that Enterprize, and whom Providence ſeems to have in a Manner ingag'd to advance in Wealth and Honour, to the Amazement of the World, and yet free from Envy,
from Jealouſy, and from any Sort of Complaints.
There is therefore no Reaſon to preſage otherwiſe than well of the Event of this Affair ; the
Bleſſings God has pour'd down upon all his
former Undertakings, ſeem to be a Security
for what is to follow. There is Reaſon to hope
for ſtill greater Bleſſings on this Project of a
Settlement in *Louiſiana,* as being equally advantagious to Religion and the State ; for the pro-
pagating of the Knowledge and Service of God
O
among

among an infinite Number of Savages, by Means
of the Miſſioners, who are to be ſent to and
maintain'd in thoſe vaſt Countries ; the Planting of the Faith in that new World, only the
Name whereof is known to us, and the Redu-
cing of it to be a Chriſtian and a *French* Province,
under the Dominion of our Auguſt Monarch,
and to the eternal Memory of his Reign, will
be the Conſequences and the Fruits of Monſieur
Crozat's Care and Expence, the Glory of his
Enterprize, the Security of the large Fortune
he has made in this Life, and what is rare a-
mong ſuch rich Men, the Earneſt of much better in the Next. Heaven grant our Hopes and
Wiſhes may be anſwer'd.

I am, &c.

The Letters Patent granted by the King of France *to M.* Crozat.

L *O U I S,* by the Grace of God, King of
    France and *Navarre :* To all who ſhall
ſee theſe preſent Letters, Greeting. The
Care we have always had to procure the Wel-
fare and Advantage of our Subjects having in-
duced us, notwithſtanding the almoſt continual
Wars which we have been obliged to ſupport
from the Beginning of our Reign, to ſeek
for all poſſible Opportunities of enlarging
and extending the Trade of our American
Colonies, *We did in the Year* 1683 *give our Orders*
                                            to

to undertake a Discovery of the Countries and Lands which are situated in the Nothern Part of America, between New France and New Mexico : *And the Sieur* de la Sale, *to whom we committed that Enterprize, having had Success enough to confirm a Belief that a Communication might be settled* from New France to the Gulph of Mexico by Means of large Rivers ; *This obliged us immediately after the Peace of* Ryswick *to give Orders for the establishing a Colony there, and maintaining a Garrison which has kept and preserved* the Possession, we had taken *in the very Year* 1683 *of the Lands, Coasts and Islands which are situated in the Gulph of Mexico, between* Carolina on *the East, and Old and New Mexico on the West.* But a new War having broke out in Europe shortly after, there was no Possibility, till now, of reaping from that new Colony the Advantages that might have been expected from thence, because the private Men, who are concerned in the Sea Trade, were all under Engagements with other Colonies, which they have been obliged to follow : And whereas upon the Information we have received concerning the Disposition and Situation of the said Countries known at present by the Name of the Province of *Louisiana,* we are of Opinion that there may be established therein a considerable Commerce, so much the more advantageous to our Kingdom in that there has hitherto been a Necessity of fetching from Foreigners the greatest Part of the Commodities which may be brought from thence, and because in Exchange thereof we need carry thither nothing but Commodities of the Growth and Manufacture of our own Kingdom ; we have resolv-

ed

ed to grant the Commerce of the Country of *Louifiana* to the *Sieur Authony Crozat* our Councellor, Secretary of the Houfhold, Crown and Revenue, to whom we entruft the Execution of this Projeĉt. We are the more readily inclined hereunto, becaufe his Zeal and the fingular Knowledge he has acquired in maritime Commerce, encourage us to hope for as good Succefs as he has hitherto had in the divers and fundry Enterprizes he has gone upon, and which have procured to our Kingdom great Quantities of Gold and Silver in fuch Conjunĉtures as have rendred them very welcome to us.

FOR THESE REASONS being defirous to fhew our Favour to him, and to regulate the Conditions upon which we mean to grant him the faid Commerce, after having deliberated this Affair in our Council, Of our certain Knowledge, full Power and Royal Authority, We by thefe Prefents, figned by our Hand, have appointed and do appoint the faid *Sieur Crozat folely to carry on a Trade in all the Lands* poffeffed by Us, and bounded by New Mexico, and by the Lands of the Englifh of Carolina, *all the Eftablifhment, Ports, Havens, Rivers, and principally the Port and Haven of the Ifle* Dauphine, *heretofore called* Maffacre ; *the River of* St. Lewis, *heretofore called* Miffifipi, *from the Edge of the Sea as far as the* Iffinois ; *together with the River of* St. Philip, *heretofore called the* Miffourys, *and of* St. Jerome, *heretofore called* Ovabache, *with all the Countries, Territories, Lakes within Land, and the Rivers which fall directly or indirectly into that Part of the River of* St. Lewis.

THE

The ARTICLES.

I. Our Pleasure is, that all the aforesaid Lands, Countries Streams, Rivers and Islands be and remain comprised under the Name of *The Government of* Louisiana, *which shall be dependant upon the General Government of New France,* to which it is subordinate ; and further, that all the Lands which we possess from the *Islinois* be united, so far as Occasion requires, to the General Government of *New France,* and become Part thereof, reserving however to Ourselves the Liberty of enlarging as We shall think fit the Extent of the Government of the said Country of *Louisiana.*

II. We grant to the said *Sieur Crozat* for Fifteen successive Years, to be reckon'd from the Day of Inrolling these presents, a Right and Power to transport all Sorts of Goods and Merchandize from *France* into the said Country of *Louisiana,* and to traffick thither as he shall think fit. We forbid all and every Person and Persons, Company and Companies of what Quality or Condition soever, and under any Pretence whatever, to trade thither, under Penalty of Confiscation of Goods, Ships, and other more severe Punishments, as Occasion shall require ; for this Purpose we order our Governours and other Officers commanding our Troops in the said Country forcibly to abet, aid and assist the Directors and Agents of the said *Sieur Crozat.*

III. We permit him to search for, open and dig all Sorts of Mines, Veins and Minerals throughout the whole Extent of the said Country of *Louisiana,* and to transport the Profits thereof into any Port of *France* during the said

Fif-

Fifteen Years; and we grant in Perpetuity to him, his Heirs, and others claiming under him or them, the Property of, in and to the Mines, Veins and Minerals which he shall bring to bear, paying us, in Lieu of all Claim, the Fifth Part of the Gold and Silver which the said *Sieur Crozat* shall cause to be transported to *France* at his own Charges into what Port he pleases, (of which Fifth we will run the Risque of the Sea and of War,) and the Tenth Part of what Effects he shall draw from the other Mines, Veins and Minerals, which Tenth he shall transfer and convey to our Magazines in the said Country of *Louisiana*.

We likewise permit him to search for precious Stones and Pearls, paying us the Fifth Part in the same Manner as is mention'd for the Gold and Silver.

We will that the said *Sieur Crozat*, his Heirs, or those claiming under him or them the perpetual Right, shall forfeit the Propriety of the said Mines, Veins and Minerals, if they discontinue the Work during three Years, and that in such Case the said Mines, Veins and Minerals shall be fully reunited to our Domaine, by Virtue of this present Article, without the Formality of any Process of Law, but only an Ordinance of Re-union from the Subdelegate of the Intendant of *New France*, who shall be in the said Country, nor do we mean that the said Penalty of Forfeiture in Default of working for three Years, be reputed a Comminatory Penalty.

IV. The said *Sieur Crozat* may vend all such Merchandize, Goods, Wares, Commodities, Arms, and Ammunition as he shall have caused

to

to be transported into the said Country and Government of *Louisiana*, as well to the *French*, as *Savages* who are or shall be there setled; nor shall any Person or Persons under any Pretence whatsoever be capable of doing the like without his Leave expressed in Writing.

V. He may purchase in the said Country, all Sorts of Furs, Skins, Leather, Wool,, and other Commodities and Effects of the said Country, and transport them to *France* during the said Fifteen Years : And as our Intention is to favour, as much as we can, our Inhabitants of *New France*, and to hinder the Lessening of their Trade, we forbid him Trafficking for Castor in the said Country under any Pretence whatsoever ; nor to Convey any from thence into our Kingdom or Foreign Countries.

VI. We Grant to the *Sieur Crozat*, his Heirs or those claiming under him or them, the Property of, in and to all Settlements and Manufactories which he shall erect or set up in the said Country for Silk, Indigo, Wooll, Leather, Mines, Veins and Minerals, as likewise the Property of, in and to the Lands which he shall cause to be Cultivated with the Mansions, Mills, and Structures which he shall cause to be built thereon, taking Grants thereof from Us, which Grants he shall obtain upon the Verbal Process and Opinion of our Governor and of the Subdelegate of the Intendant of *New France* in the said Country, to be by him Reported unto Us.

We will that the said *Sieur Crozat*, his Heirs, or those claiming under him or them, shall keep in Repair the said Settlements, Manufactures, Lands and Mills ; and in Default thereof during the Space of three Years, he and they shall

O 4   Forfeit

Forfeit the fame, and the faid Settlements, Manufactories, Lands and Mills ſhall be Re-united to our Domaine fully and amply, and in the fame Manner as is mentioned above in the Third Article concerning the Mines, Veins and Minerals.

VII. Our Edicts, Ordinances and Cuſtoms, and the Uſages of the Mayoralty and Shree-valty of *Paris*, ſhall be obſerved for Laws and Cuſtoms in the faid Country of *Louiſiana*.

VIII. The faid Sieur *Crozat* ſhall be oblig'd to fend to the faid Country of *Louiſiana* Two Ships every Year, which he ſhall cauſe to fet out in the proper Seaſon, in each of which Ships he ſhall cauſe to be imbark'd, without paying any Freight, 25 Tun of Victuals, Effects and neceſ-fary Ammunition, for the Maintenance of the Garriſon and Forts of the *Louiſiana* ; and in Cafe we ſhould cauſe to be laden above the faid 25 Tun in each Ship, we confent to pay the Freight to the faid Sieur *Crozat*, at the common Mercantile Rates.

He ſhall be oblig'd to convey our Officers of *Louiſiana* in the Ships which he ſhall fend thither, and to furniſh them with Subſiſtance and a Captain's Table for 30 Sols per Day, which we will cauſe to be paid for each.

He ſhall likewiſe give Paſſage in the faid Ships, to the Soldiers, which we ſhall pleaſe to fend to the faid Country ; and we will cauſe the ne-ceſſary Proviſions for their Subſiſtance to be furniſh'd to him, or will pay him for them at the fame Price as is paid to the Purveyor-Gene-ral of our Marine.

He ſhall be furthermore oblig'd to fend on Board each Ship, which he ſhall cauſe to fet out
for

for the said Country, Ten young Men or Women, at his own Election.

IX. We will cause to be deliver'd out of our Magazines to the said Sieur *Crozat*, 10000 Weight of Gunpowder every Year, which he shall pay us for at the Price that it shall cost us, and this for so long Time as the present Privilege shall last.

X. The Wares and Merchandize which the said Sieur *Crozat* shall consign to the said Country of *Louisiana* shall be exempt from all Duties of Exportation, laid or to be laid, on Condition, that his Directors, Deputies or Clerks, shall engage to give within the Space of a Year, to be reckon'd from the Date thereof, a Certificate of their Unlading in the said Country of *Louisiana*; under Penalty, in Case of Contravention, to pay the Quadruple of the Duties, reserving to our selves the Power of giving him a longer Respite in such Cases and Occurrences as we shall think proper.

XI. And as for the Goods and Merchandize, which the Sieur *Crozat* shall cause to be brought from the said Country of *Louisiana*, and upon his Account, into the Ports of our Kingdom, and shall afterwards cause to be transported into Foreign Countries, they shall pay no Duties either of Importation or Exportation, and shall be deposited in the Custom-House, Warehouses of Ports where they shall arrive, until they be taken away ; and when the Deputies and Clerks of the said Sieur *Crozat* shall be minded to cause them to be transported in Foreign Countries, either by Sea or Land, they shall be oblig'd to give Security to bring within a certain Time, a Certificate from the
last

laft Office, containing what they Exported there, and another Certificate of their unlading in Foreign Countries.

XII. In Cafe the faid *Sieur Crozat* be obliged, for the furtherance of his Commerce to fetch from Foreign Countries fome Goods and Merchandize of Foreign Manufacture, in order to T R A N S P O R T them into the faid Country of *Louifiana*. He fhall make Us Acquainted therewith, and lay before Us States thereof ; upon which we, if we think fit, will Grant him our Particular Permiffion with Exemptions from all Duties of Importation and Exportation, Provided the faid Goods and Merchandize be Depofited afterwards in our Cuftom-houfe Ware-houfes until they be Laden in the Ships of the faid *Sieur Crozat*, who fhall be obliged to bring in one Year, to be reckoned from the Day of the Date hereof, a Certificate of their unlading in the faid Country of *Louifiana*, under Penalty, in Cafe of Contravention, to pay quadruple the Duties : Referving to our felves, in like Manner, the Liberty of granting to the faid *Sieur Crozat*, a longer Refpite, if it be neceffary.

XIII. The Feluccaes, Canoes, and other Veffels belonging to us, and which are in the faid Country of *Louifiana*, fhall ferve for loading, unloading and tranfporting the Effects of the faid *Sieur Crozat*, who fhall be bound to keep them in good Condition, and after the Expiration of the faid Fifteen Years fhall reftore them, or a like Number of equal Bulk and Goodnefs, to our Governor in the faid Country.

XIV. If for the Cultures and Plantations which the faid *Sieur Crozat* is minded to make

he

he finds it proper to have Blacks in the said Country of the *Louisiana*, he may send a Ship every Year to trade for them directly upon the Coast of *Guinea*, taking Permission from the *Guinea* Company so to do, he may sell those Blacks, to the Inhabitants of the Colony of *Louisiana* ; and we forbid all other Companies and Persons whatsoever, under any Pretence whatsoever, to introduce Blacks or Traffick for them in the said Country, nor shall the said *Sieur Crozat* carry any Blacks else where.

XV. He shall not send any Ships into the said Country of *Louisiana* but directly from *France*, and he shall Cause the said Ships to Return thither again; the whole under Pain of Confiscation and Forfieture of the Present Priviledge.

XVI. THE said *Sieur Crozat* shall be obliged, after the Expiration of the first nine Years of this Grant, to Pay the Officers and the Garrison which shall be in the said Country During the Six last Years of the Continuance of this Present Priviledge : The said *Sieur Crozat* may in that Time propose and nominate the Officers, as Vacancies shall fall, and such Officers, shall be Confirmed by us, if we approve of them.

Given at *FONTAINBLEAU* the Fourteenth Day of September in the Year of Grace 1712. And of Our Reign the 70th.

SIGNED *LOUIS*
    By the KING

                    PHELIPEAUX, &c.

Register'd at *PARIS* in the Parliament, the Four and Twentieth of September, 1712.

T H E

I N D E X.

INDEX.

INDEX.

Mea-

INDEX.

Salt

INDEX.

F I N I S.